THE START KOREAN ALPHABET Writing Workbook

한글 자음, 모음 & 기초 단어

Table of Contents

Chapter1. Consonants

Chapter2. Vowels

Chapter3. Making Words

Chapter4. Korean Word Cards

Learning Korean Alphabet Videos

자음 알기

Learning Korean Consonants Video

모음 알기

Learning Korean Vowels Video

자음 구별하기

Learning Consonants Special Tips Video

모음 구별하기

Learning Vowels Special Tips Video

Features of this workbook

1. Unique Korean Characters

Easily and enjoyably learn the shapes and names of Korean alphabet through Korean characters. Watch videos and practice writing Korean alphabet in the workbook.

2. Writing Challenge

Enjoy writing consonants and vowels through this writing challenge.
Gradually take on the challenge of writing in smaller spaces.

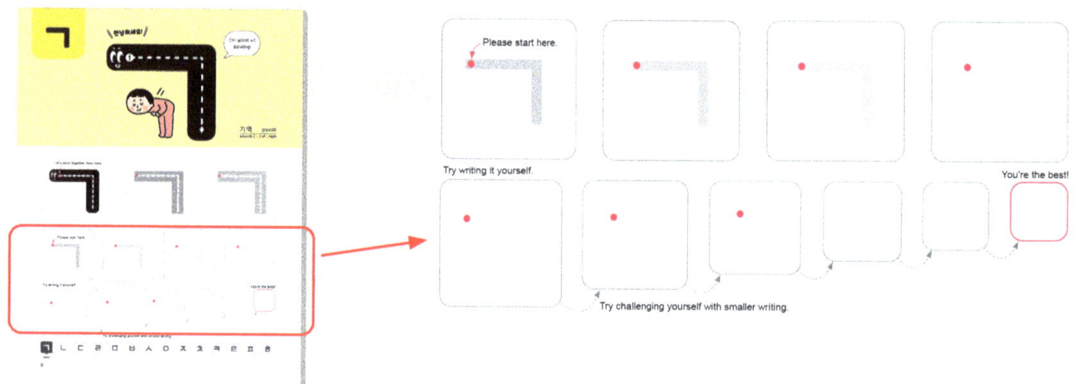

3. Coloring Korean Words

Word coloring aids beginners in learning Korean words in a stress-free manner.
Learn Korean words by coloring pictures and words.

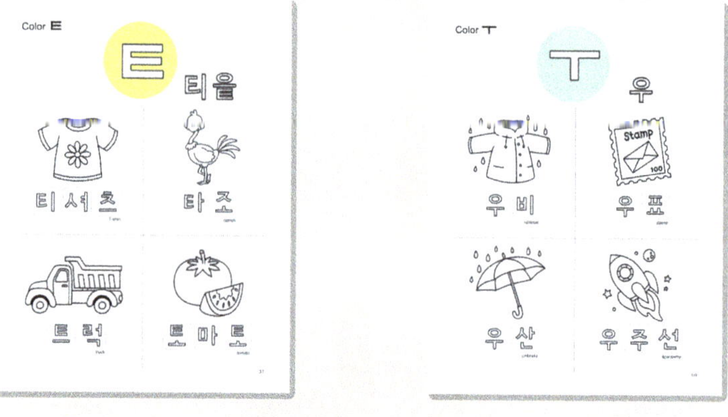

4. Making Korean Word Cards

Word cards for learning Korean are designed to be carried anywhere. Color, fold, cut, and make your own Korean word cards.

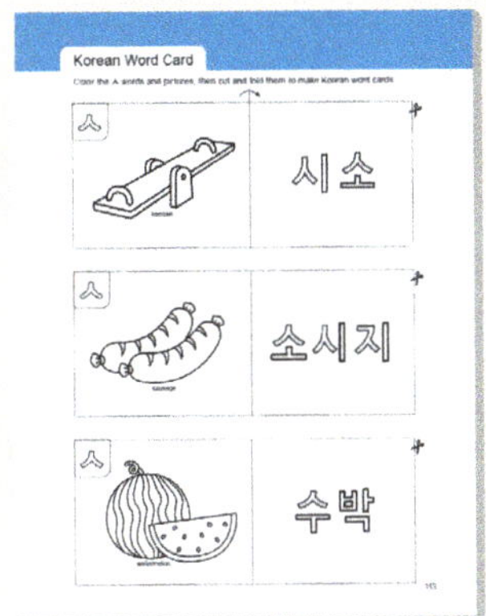

5. Exclusive to This Workbook! 'Special tips'

Tips for learning Korean easily by comparing the shapes of consonants and vowels are included! Get a better understanding by watching the videos featuring characters to assist in writing letters.

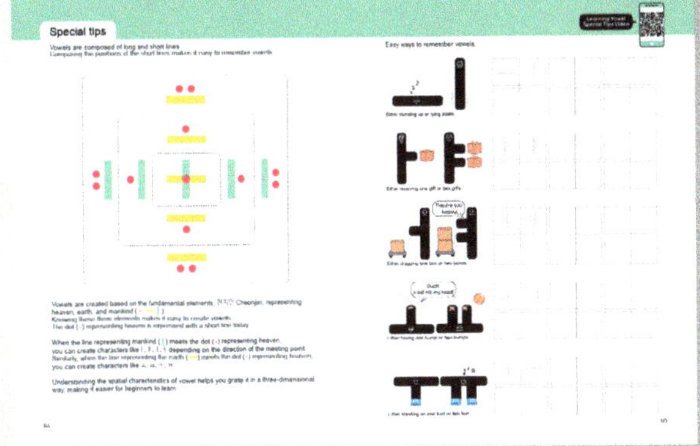

6. Learning Korean with Videos

Master Korean alphabet by watching videos of Korean letter animated characters. Of course, fun is a bonus!

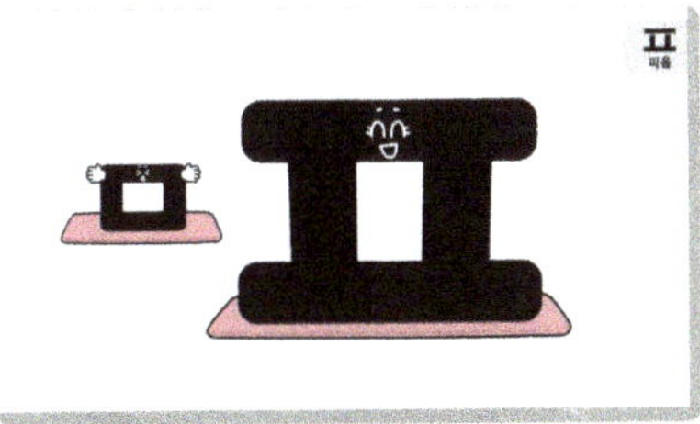

Chapter1

Consonants

Learning Korean Consonants Video

Would you like to meet consonant animated characters?

ㄱ
기역 giyeok
ㄴ
니은 nieun
ㄷ
디귿 digeut
ㄹ
리을 rieul
ㅁ
미음 mieum
ㅂ
비읍 bieup
ㅅ
시옷 siot
ㅇ
이응 ieung
ㅈ
지읒 jieut
ㅊ
치읓 chieut
ㅋ
키읔 kieuk
ㅌ
티읕 tieut
ㅍ
피읖 pieup
ㅎ
히읗 hieut

ㄱ

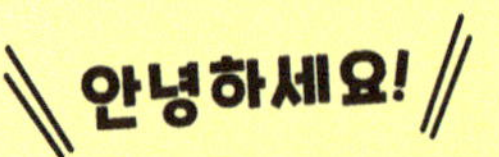

I'm good at bowing!

기역 giyeok
sounds [g] of grape

Let's write together from here.

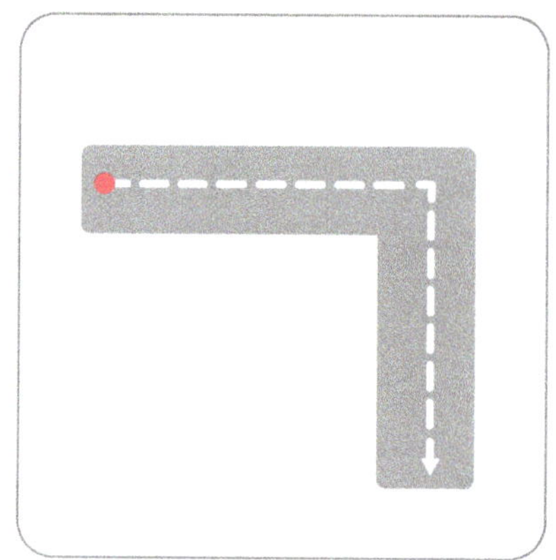
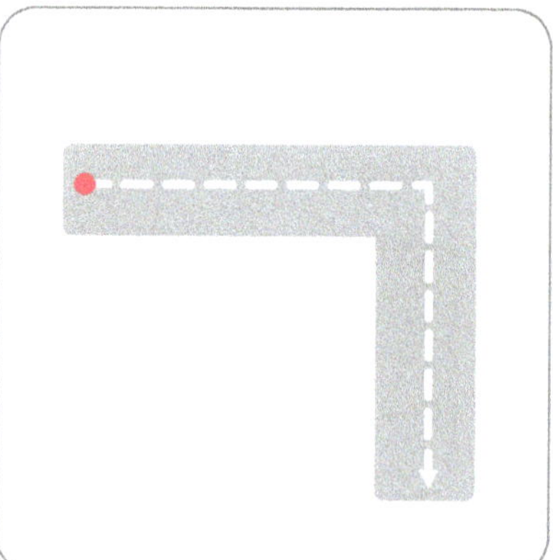

Please start here.

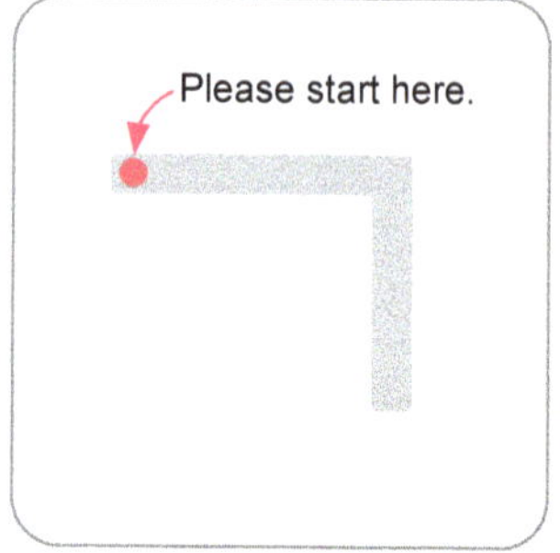
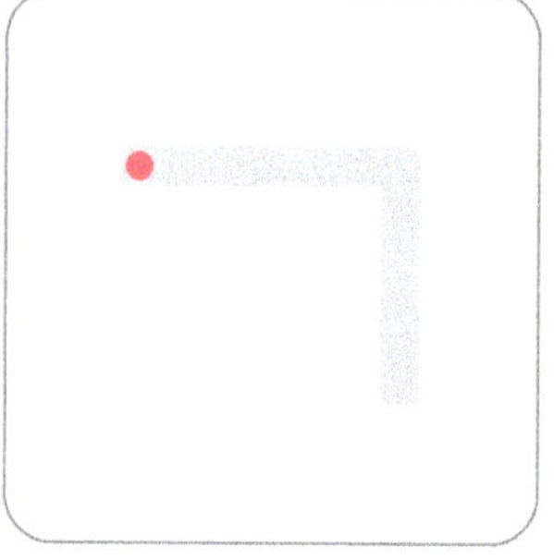

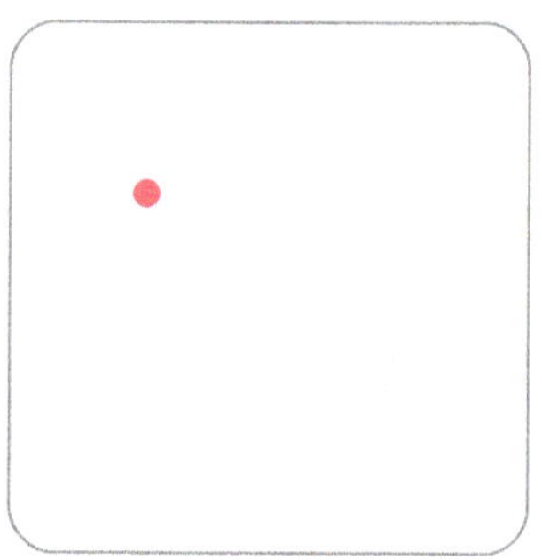

Try writing it yourself.

You're the best!

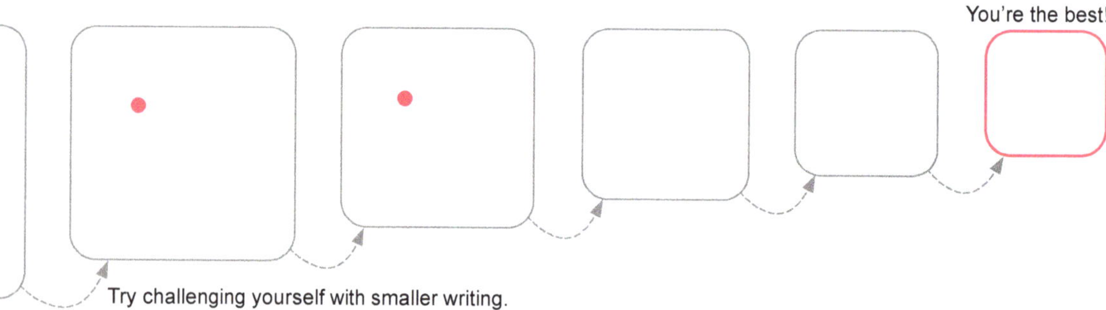

Try challenging yourself with smaller writing.

ㄱ ㄴ ㄷ ㄹ ㅁ ㅂ ㅅ ㅇ ㅈ ㅊ ㅋ ㅌ ㅍ ㅎ

Here!

Color ㄱ

ㄱ

기역

기 차

train

가 지

eggplant

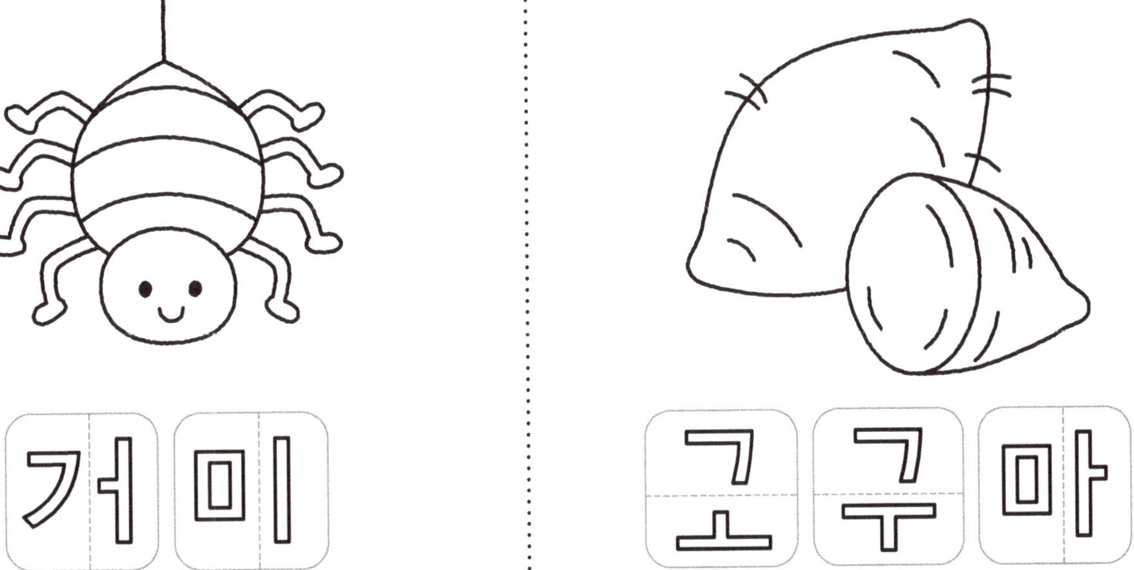

거 미

spider

고 구 마

sweet potato

ㄴ

Am I a caterpillar, too?
No! I'm nieun.
1

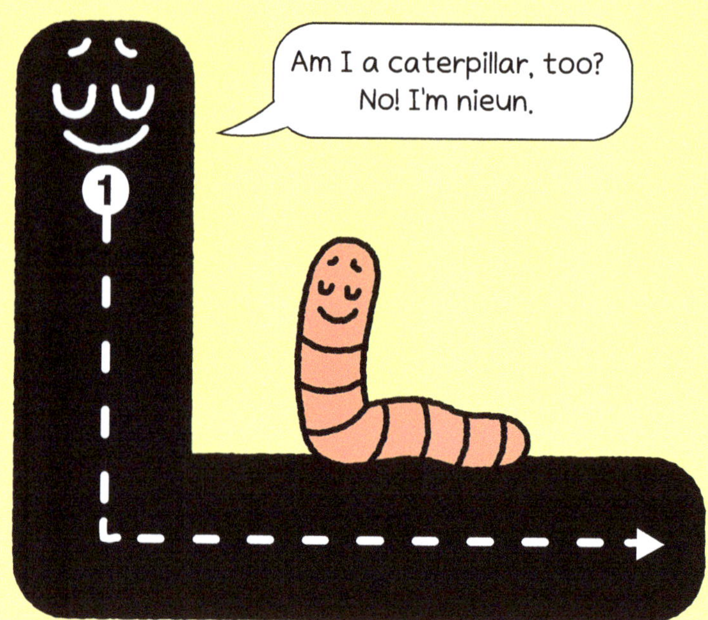

니은 nieun

sounds [n] of nose

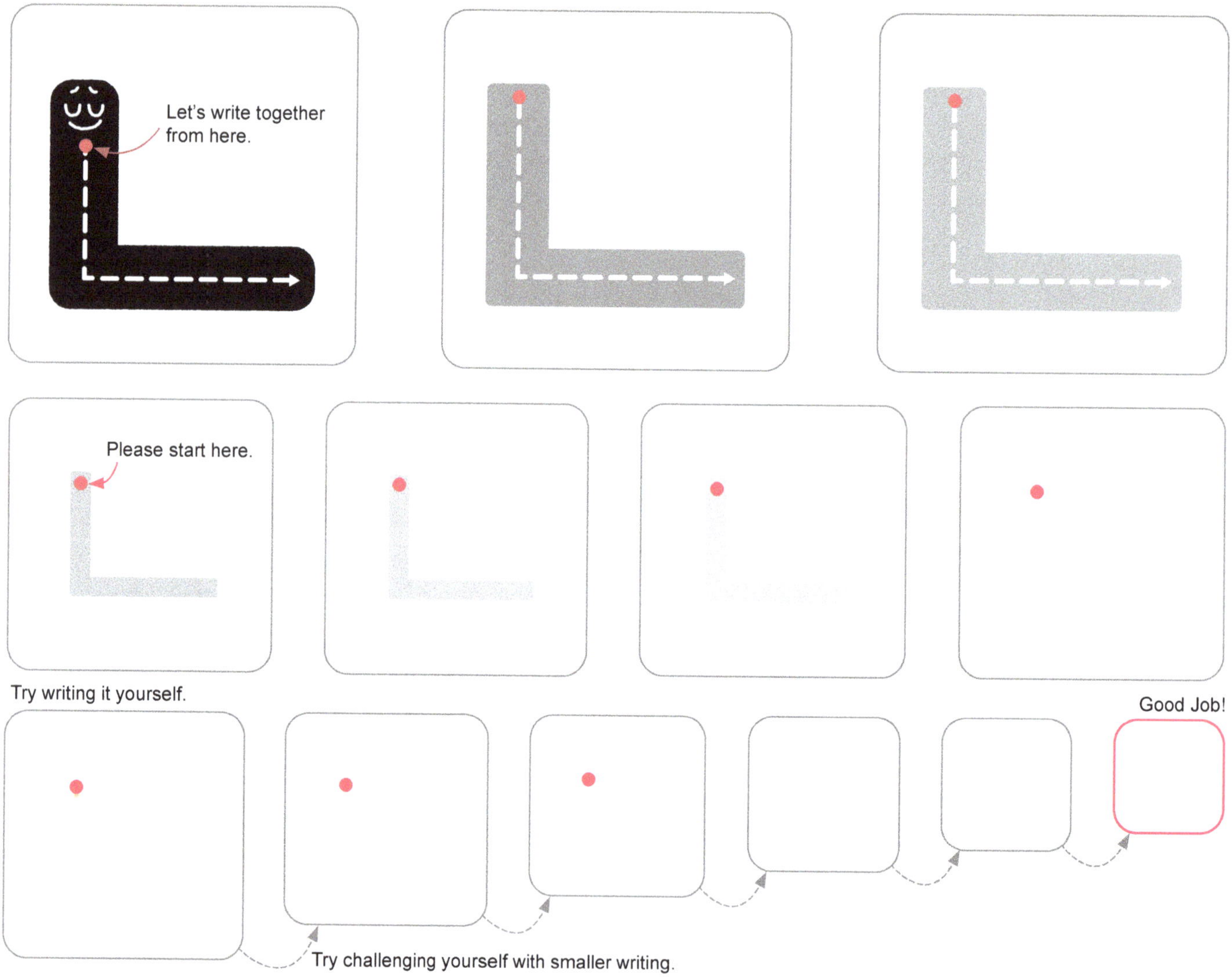
Let's write together from here.
Please start here.
Try writing it yourself.
Good Job!
Try challenging yourself with smaller writing.

ㄱ ㄴ ㄷ ㄹ ㅁ ㅂ ㅅ ㅇ ㅈ ㅊ ㅋ ㅌ ㅍ ㅎ

Here!

Color ㄴ

ㄴ

니은

니트

sweater

나비

butterfly

너구리

raccoon

누나

older sister

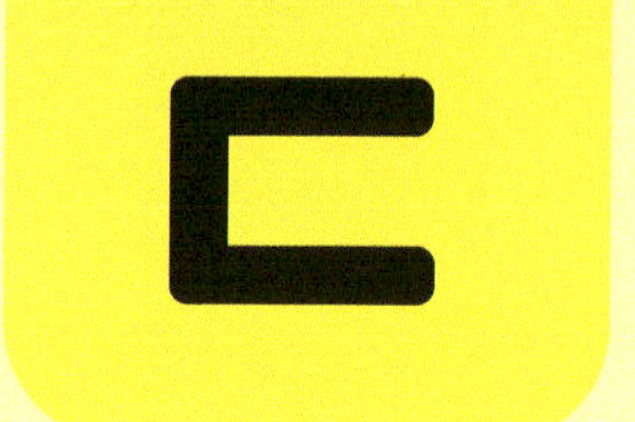

Is the alligator's mouth bigger, or is digeut's mouth bigger?

디귿 digeut

sounds [d] of dog

Let's write together from here.

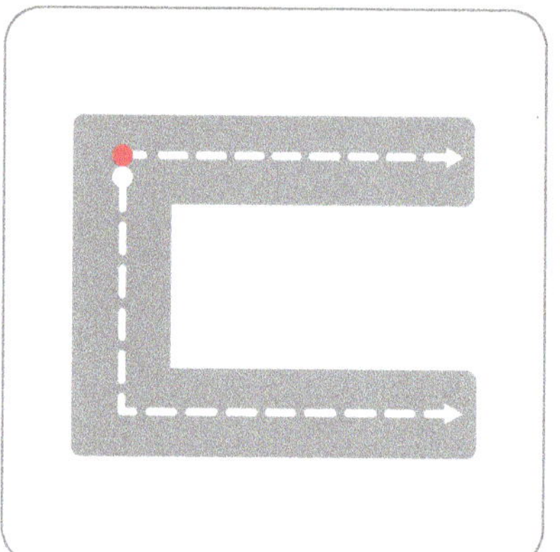

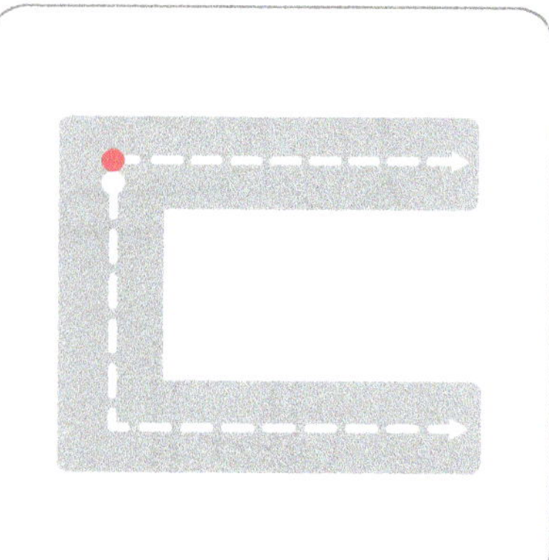

Please start here.

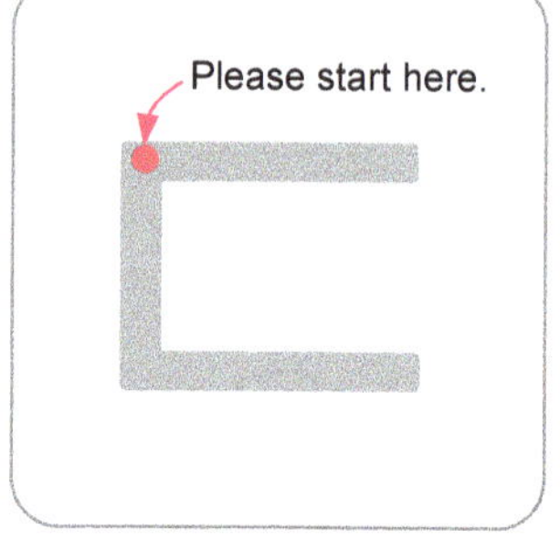

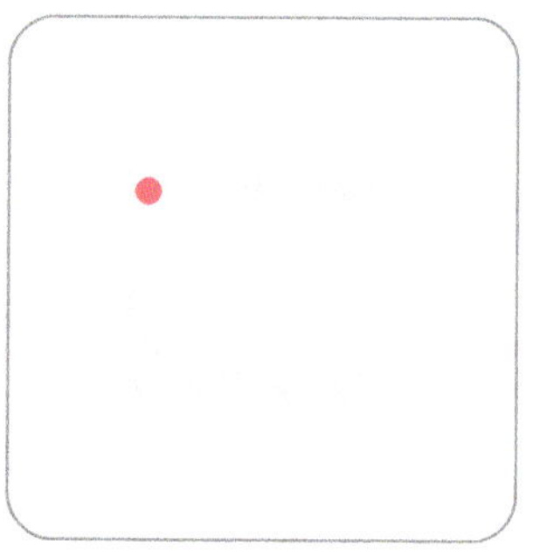

Try writing it yourself.

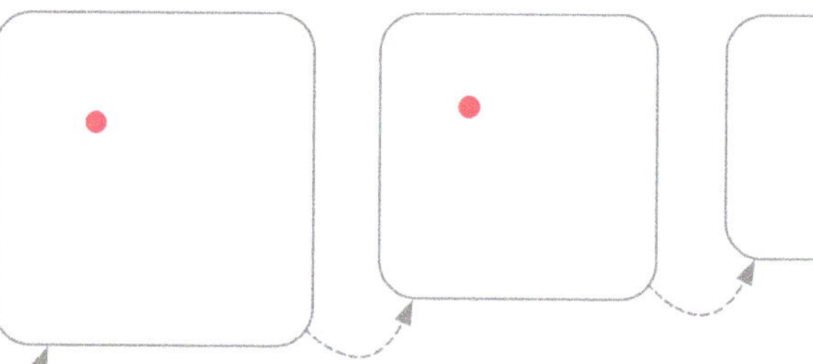

Well done!

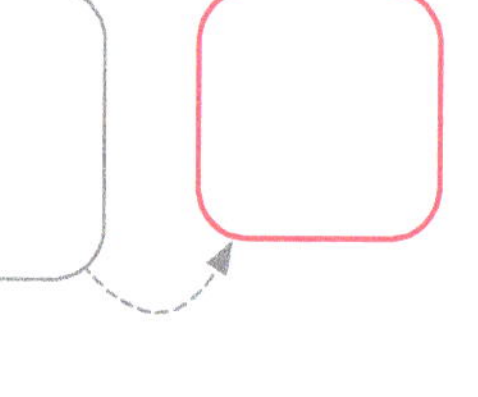

Try challenging yourself with smaller writing.

ㄱ ㄴ ㄷ ㄹ ㅁ ㅂ ㅅ ㅇ ㅈ ㅊ ㅋ ㅌ ㅍ ㅎ

Here!

Color ㄷ

ㄷ

디귿

다리

leg

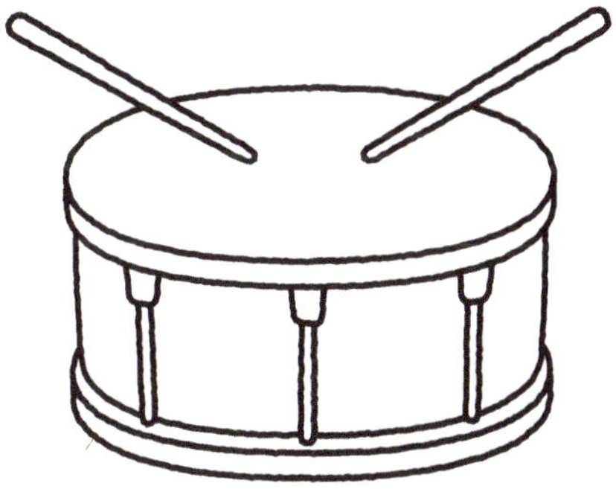

드럼

drum

도로

road

두더지

mole

Don't I look like
a squiggly snake?
But I'm rieul.

리을 rieul

sounds [r] of ribbon

Let's write together from here.

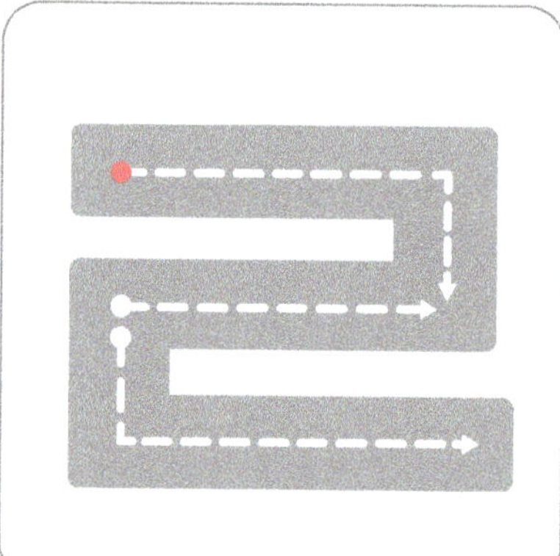

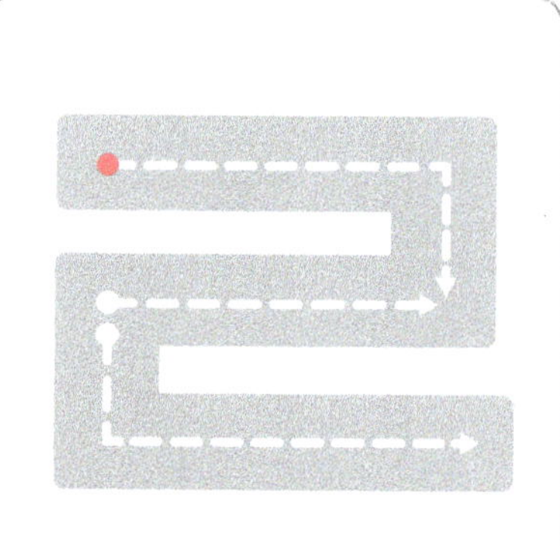

Please start here.

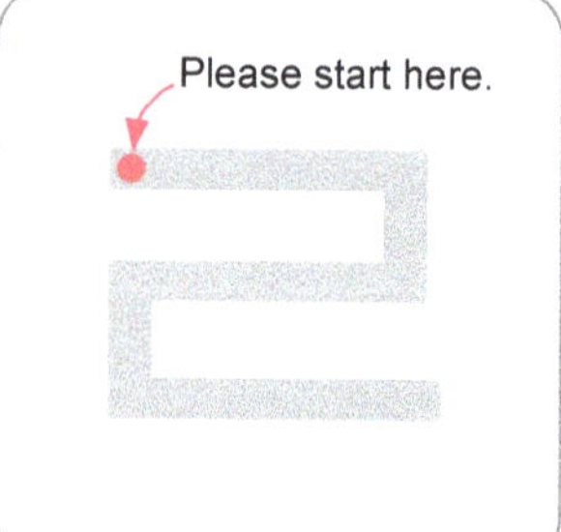

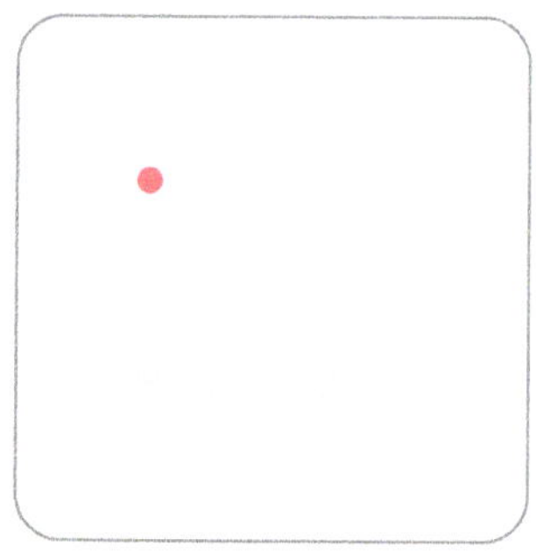

Try writing it yourself.

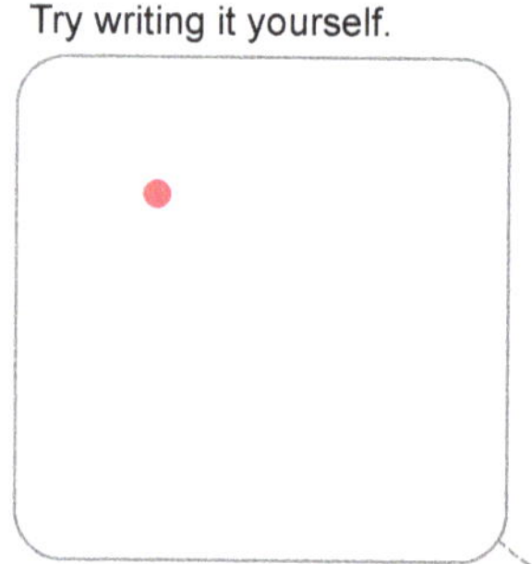

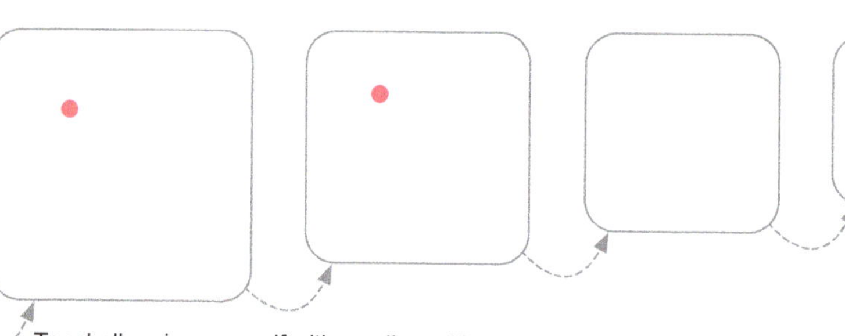

Awesome!

Try challenging yourself with smaller writing.

ㄱ ㄴ ㄷ ㄹ ㅁ ㅂ ㅅ ㅇ ㅈ ㅊ ㅋ ㅌ ㅍ ㅎ

Here!

Color ㄹ

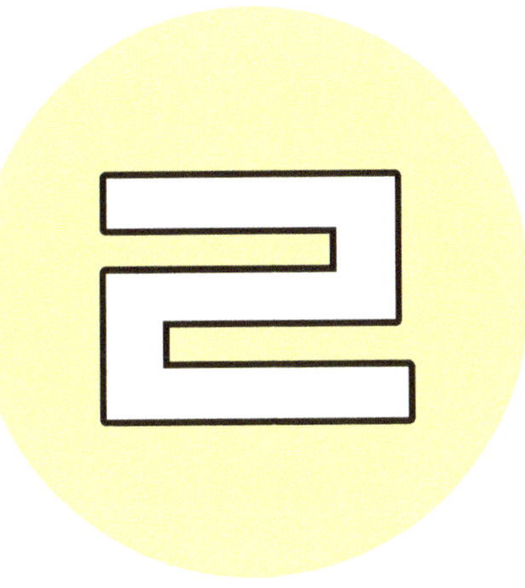

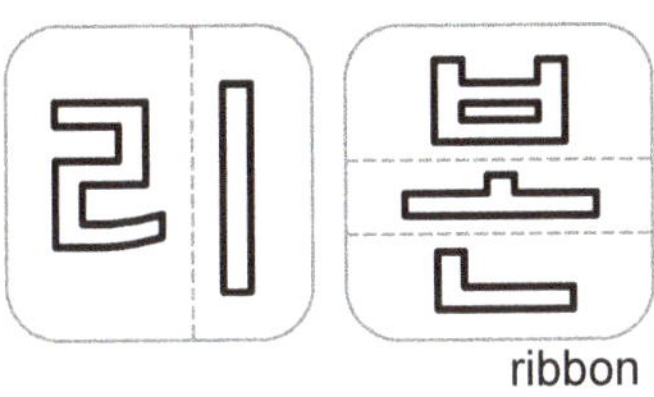

ribbon

ramyeon

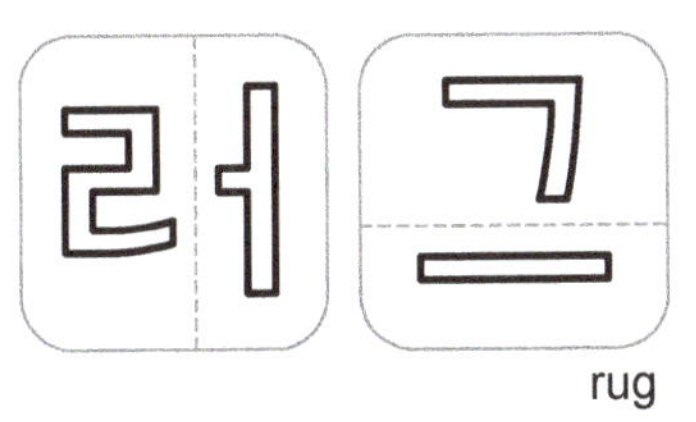

rug

로봇

robot

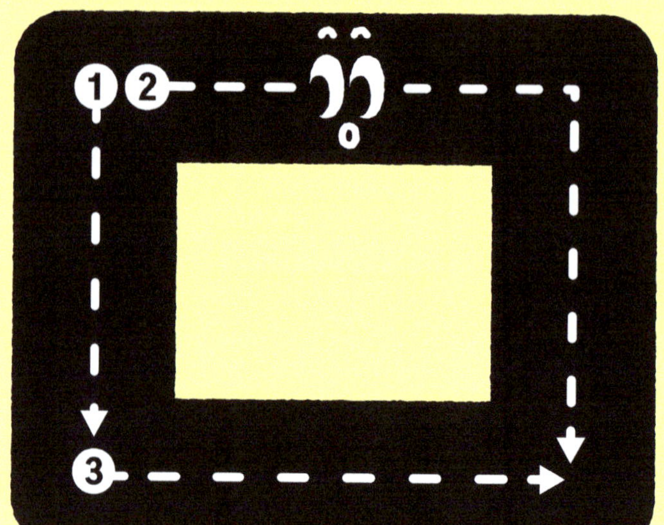

I wonder what's inside that square box that looks like me.

미음 mieum

sounds [m] of mom

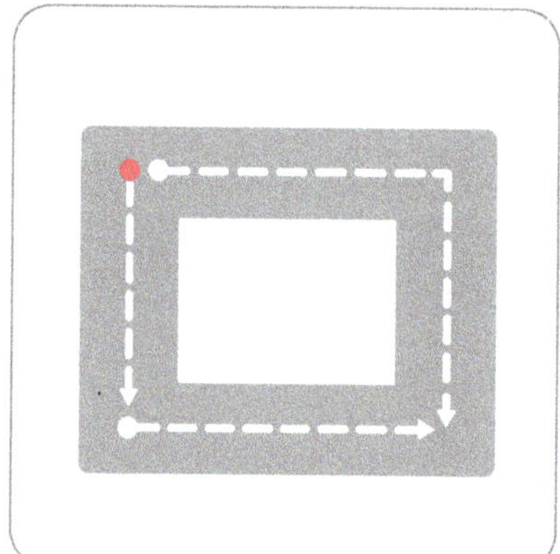

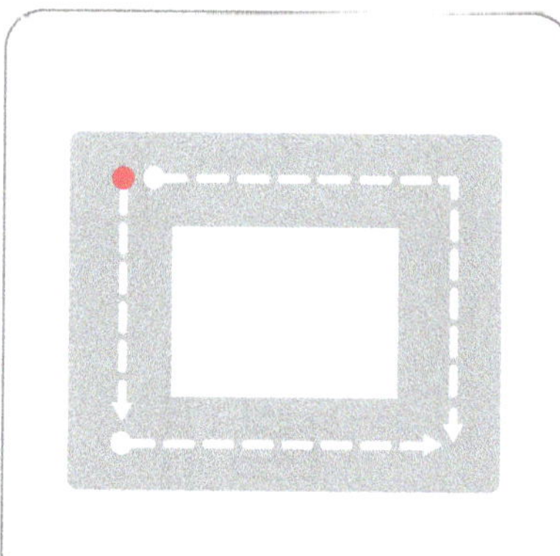

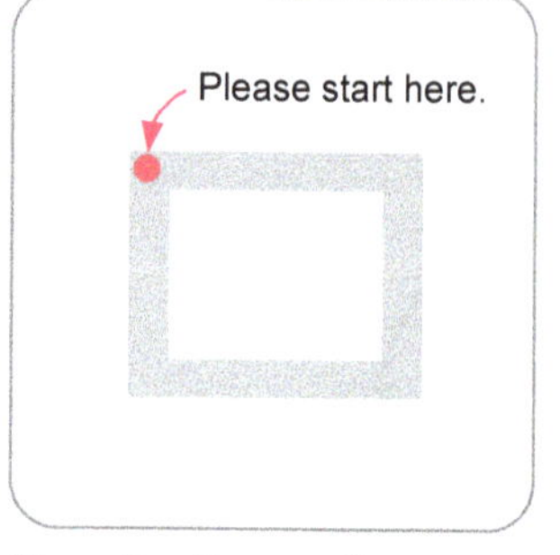

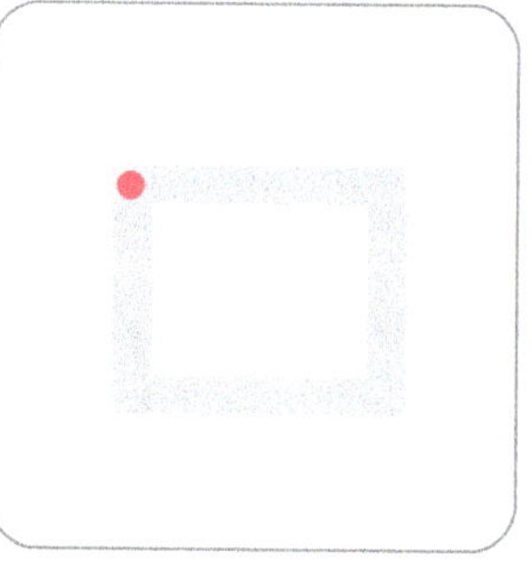

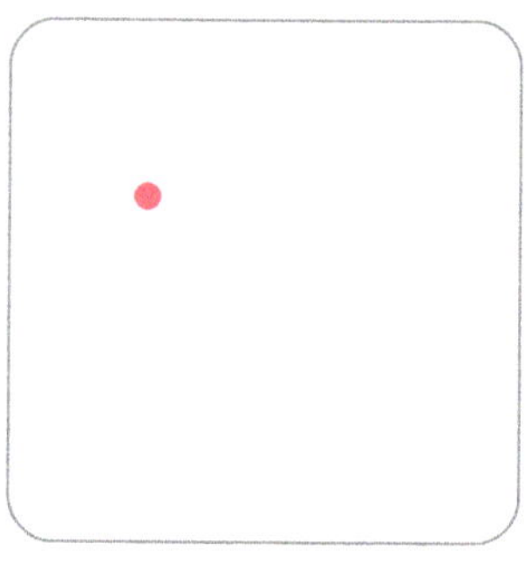

Try writing it yourself.

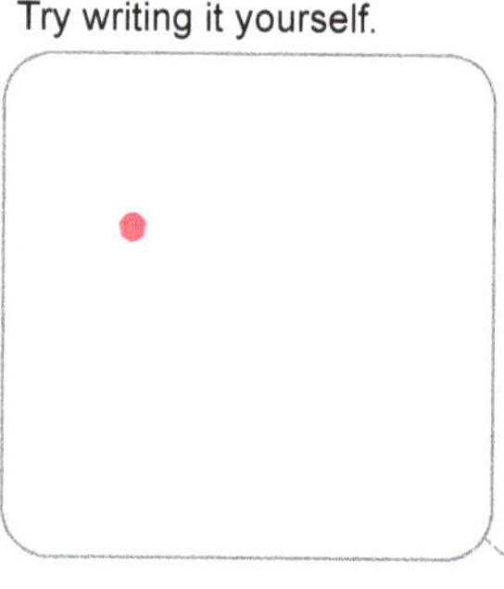

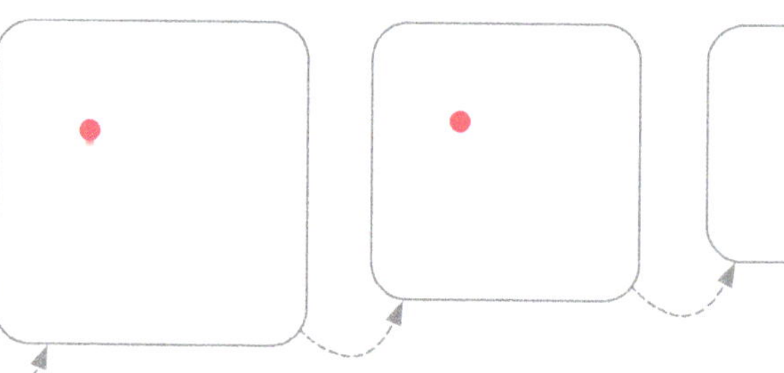

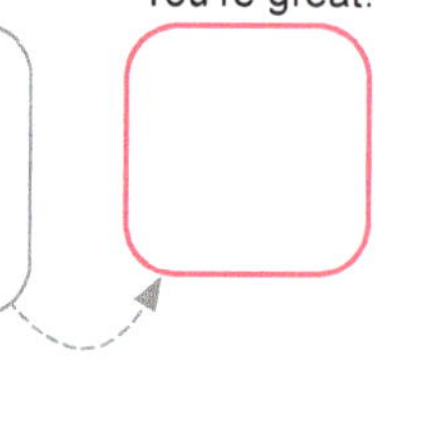

Try challenging yourself with smaller writing.

ㄱ ㄴ ㄷ ㄹ ㅁ ㅂ ㅅ ㅇ ㅈ ㅊ ㅋ ㅌ ㅍ ㅎ

Here!

Color ㅁ

ㅁ

미음

마이크

microphone

머리

head

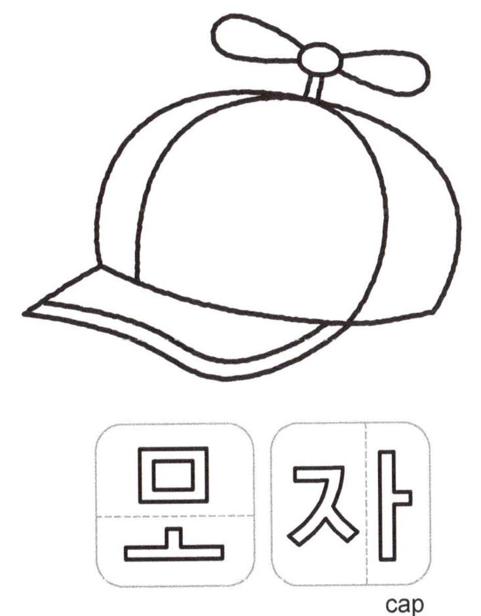

모자

cap

무지개

rainbow

ㅂ

Hmph! I'm angry, and that's why horns grew on my head!

비읍 bieup

sounds [b] of bucket

Let's write together from here.

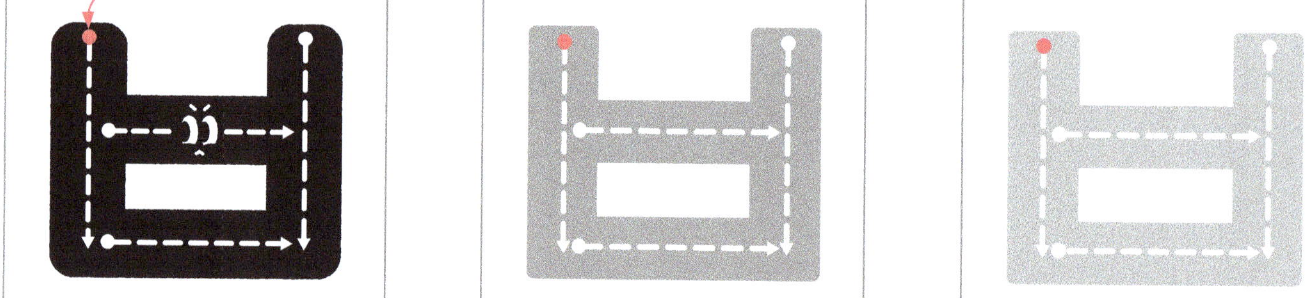

Please start here.

Try writing it yourself.

Fantastic!

Try challenging yourself with smaller writing.

ㄱ ㄴ ㄷ ㄹ ㅁ ㅂ ㅅ ㅇ ㅈ ㅊ ㅋ ㅌ ㅍ ㅎ

Here!

Color ㅂ

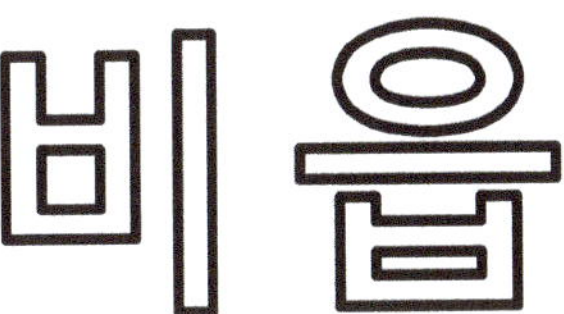

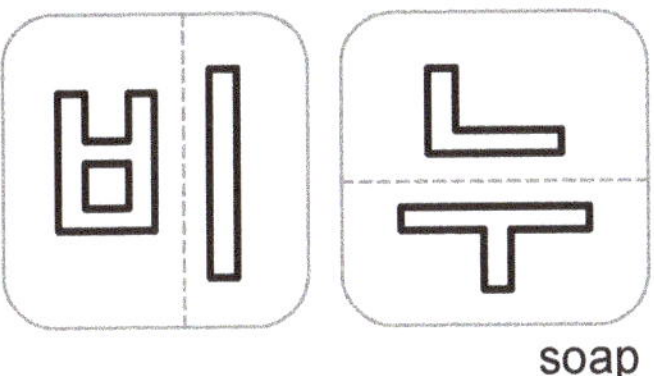

soap

바나나

banana

bus

boat

Let's write together from here.

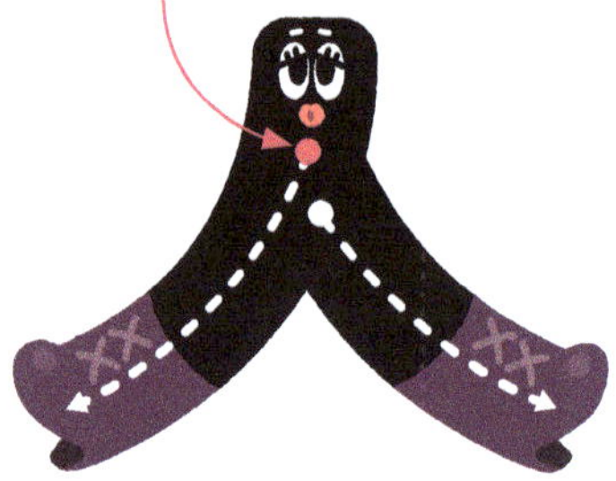

Please start here.

Try writing it yourself.

Excellent!

Try challenging yourself with smaller writing.

ㄱ ㄴ ㄷ ㄹ ㅁ ㅂ ㅅ ㅇ ㅈ ㅊ ㅋ ㅌ ㅍ ㅎ

Here!

Color ㅅ

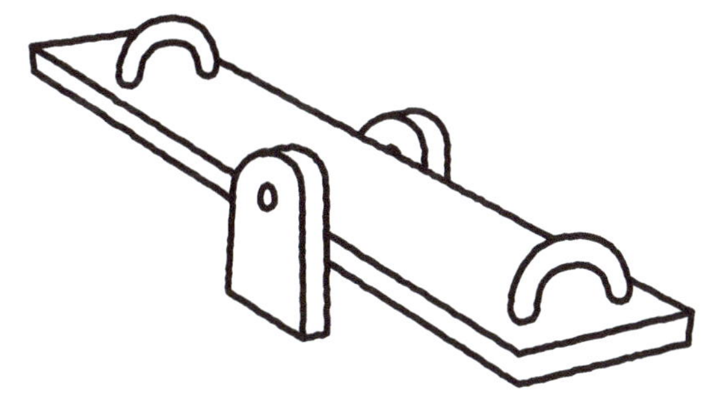

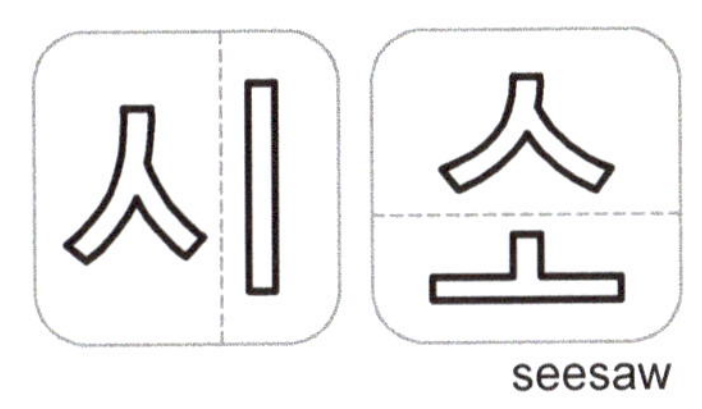

seesaw

ladder

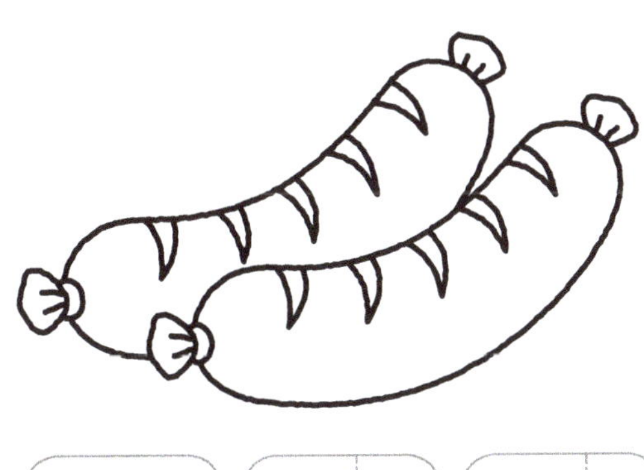

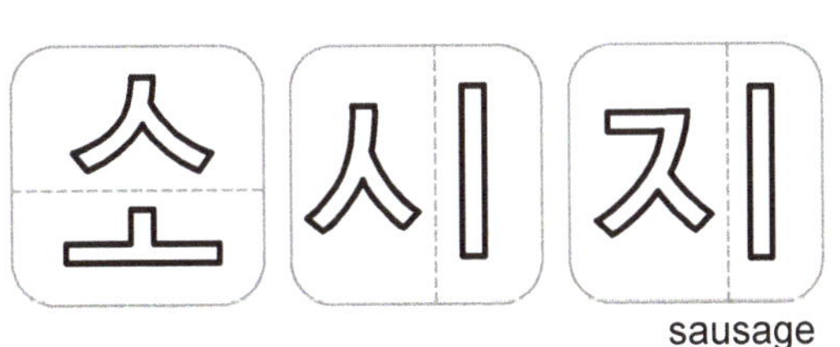

sausage

watermelon

ㅇ

I like to roll quietly without making a sound. Oh, dear. I'm so dizzy.

이응 ieung

Ieung is a silent consonant. Therefore, when consonants and vowels are combined, only the sound of the vowel is heard.

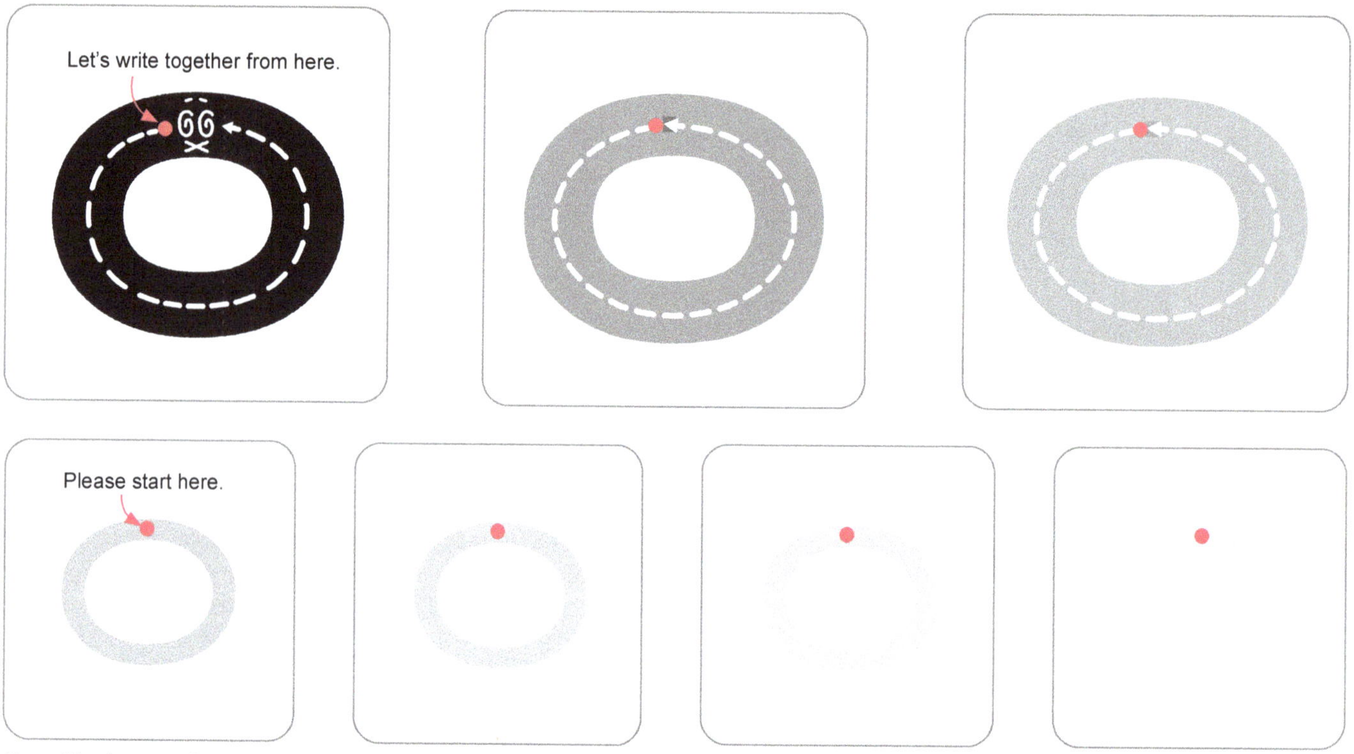

Let's write together from here.

Please start here.

Try writing it yourself.

You're the best!

Try challenging yourself with smaller writing.

ㄱ ㄴ ㄷ ㄹ ㅁ ㅂ ㅅ ㅇ ㅈ ㅊ ㅋ ㅌ ㅍ ㅎ

Here!

Color ㅇ

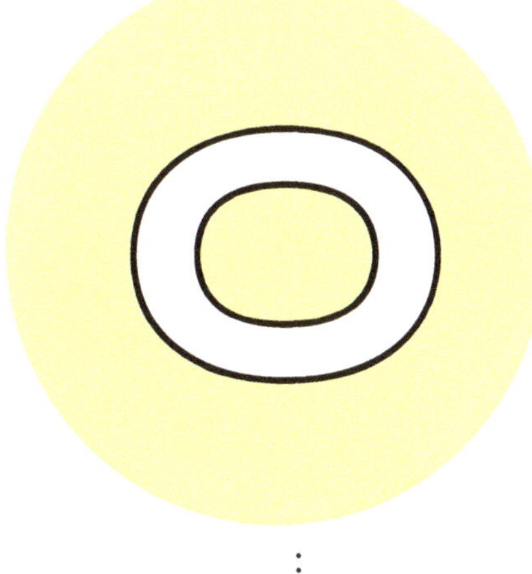

이마

forehead

아기

baby

오리

duck

우유

milk

ㅈ

I have long hair and long legs. Aren't I a beauty?

지읒 jieut

sounds [j] of jelly

Let's write together from here.

Please start here.

Try writing it yourself.

Good Job!

Try challenging yourself with smaller writing.

ㄱ ㄴ ㄷ ㄹ ㅁ ㅂ ㅅ ㅇ ㅈ ㅊ ㅋ ㅌ ㅍ ㅎ

Here!

Color ㅈ

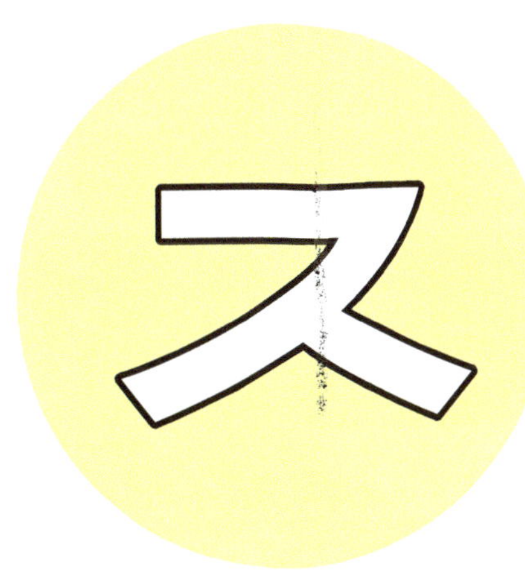

지읒

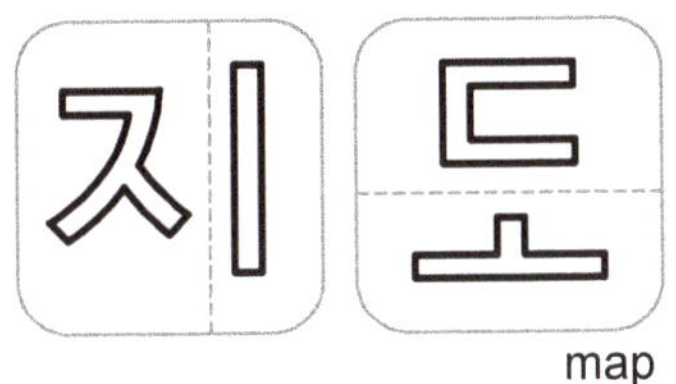

map

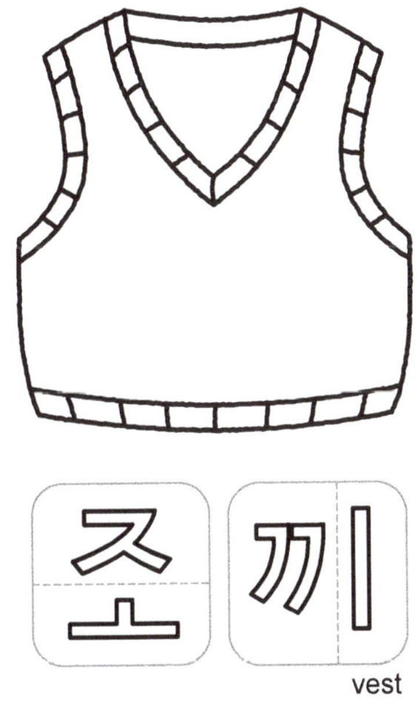

ㅊ

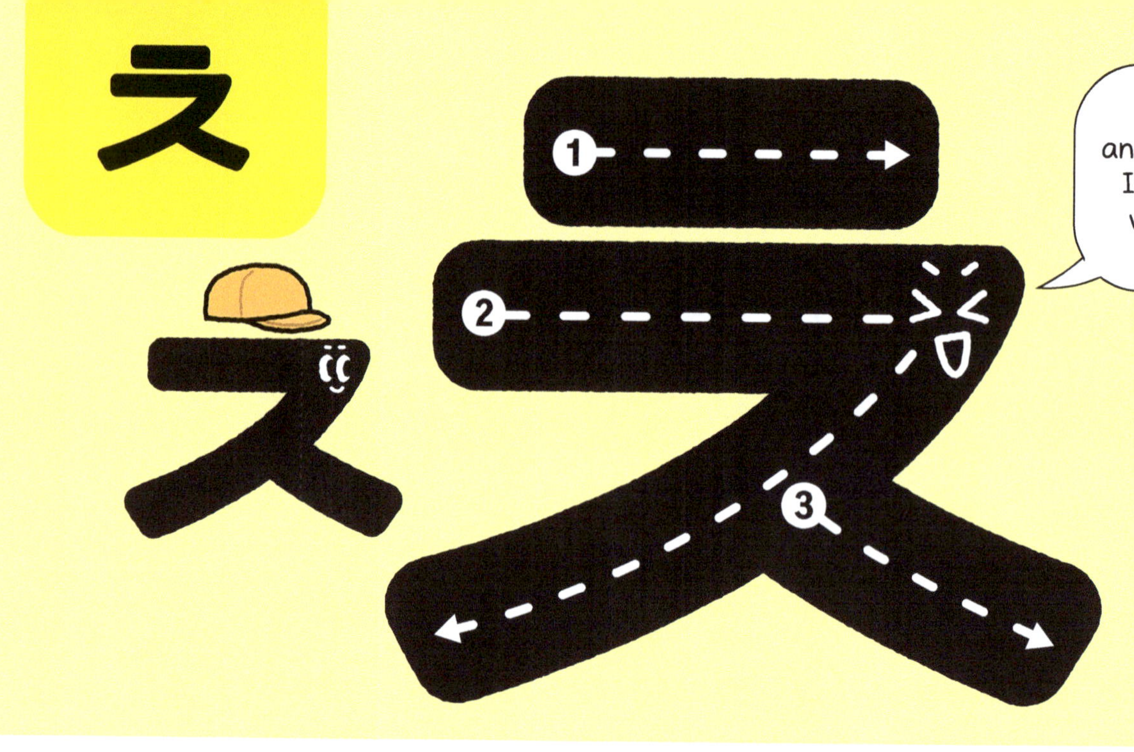

I also have long hair and long legs, just like 'ㅈ'. I even adorned myself with a stylish hat like a true trendsetter.

치읓 chieut

sounds [ch] of chicken

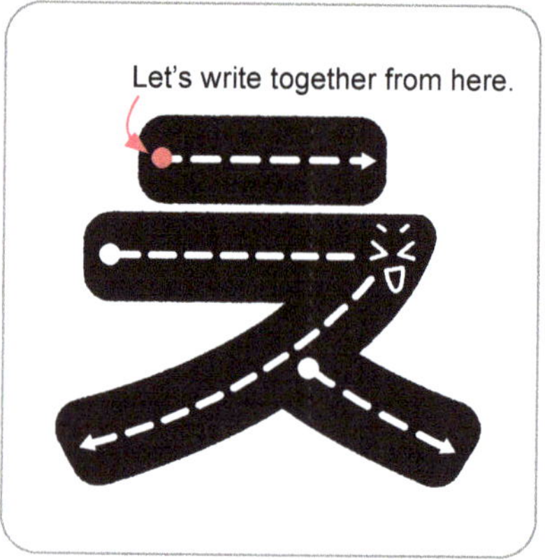

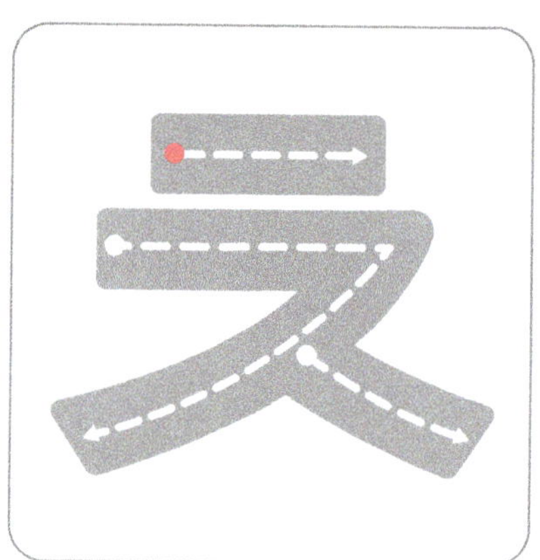

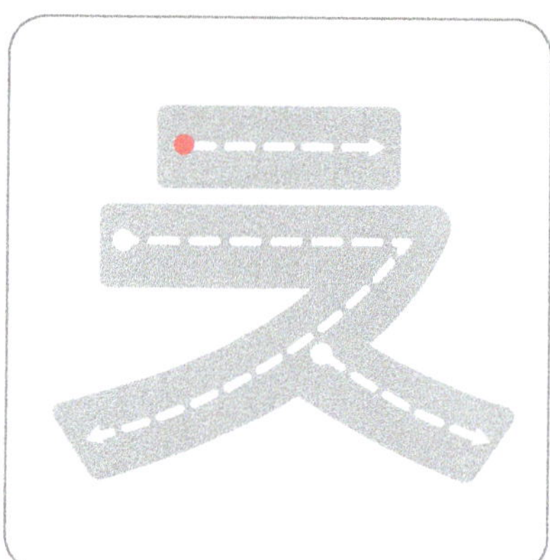

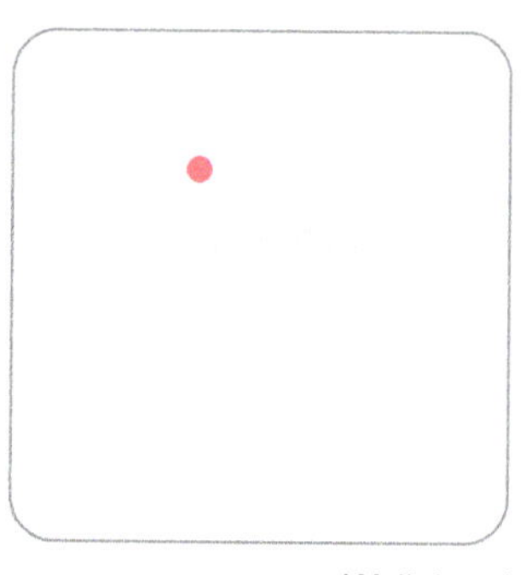

Try writing it yourself.

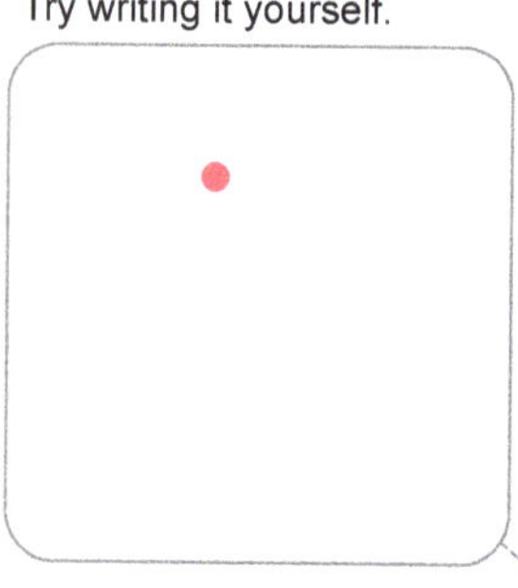

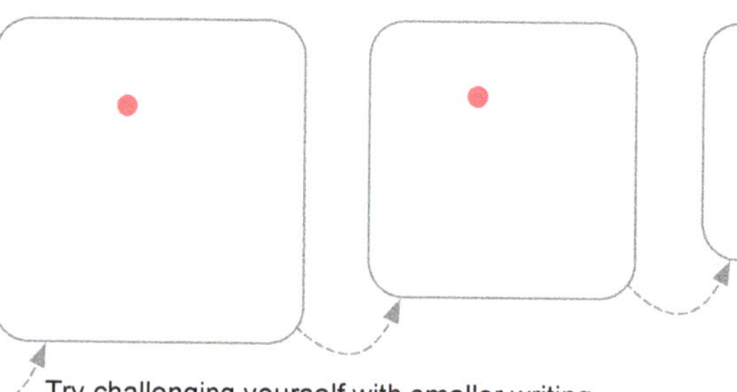

Well done!

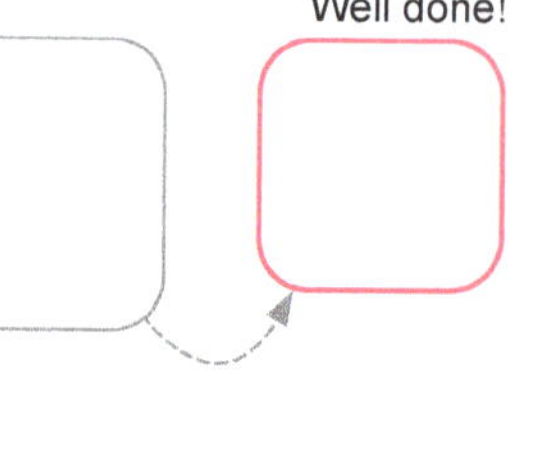

Try challenging yourself with smaller writing.

ㄱ ㄴ ㄷ ㄹ ㅁ ㅂ ㅅ ㅇ ㅈ  

Here!

Color ㅊ

치읓

cheese

차

car

chocolate

soccer ball

ㅋ

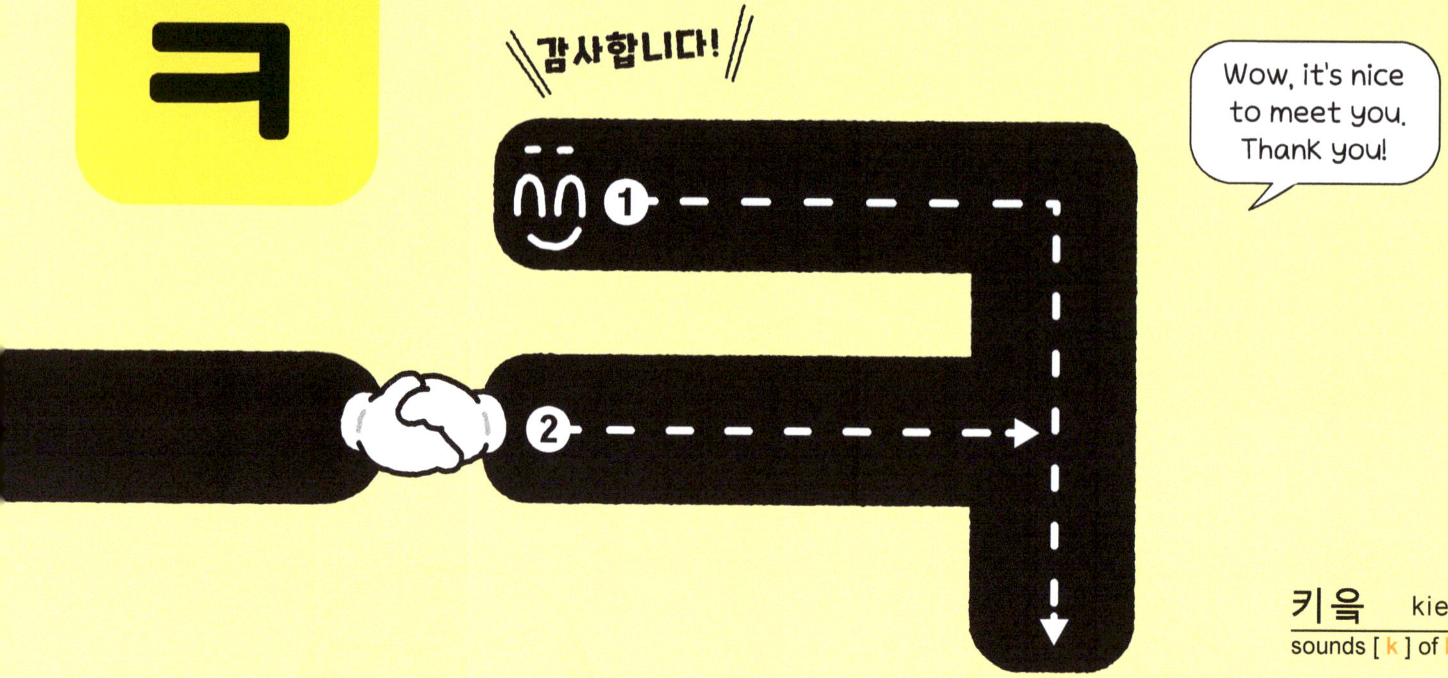

\\감사합니다!//

Wow, it's nice to meet you. Thank you!

① ②

키읔 kieuk

sounds [k] of key

Let's write together from here.

Please start here.

Try writing it yourself.

Awesome!

Try challenging yourself with smaller writing.

ㄱ ㄴ ㄷ ㄹ ㅁ ㅂ ㅅ ㅇ ㅈ ㅊ ㅋ ㅌ ㅍ ㅎ

Here!

Color ㅋ

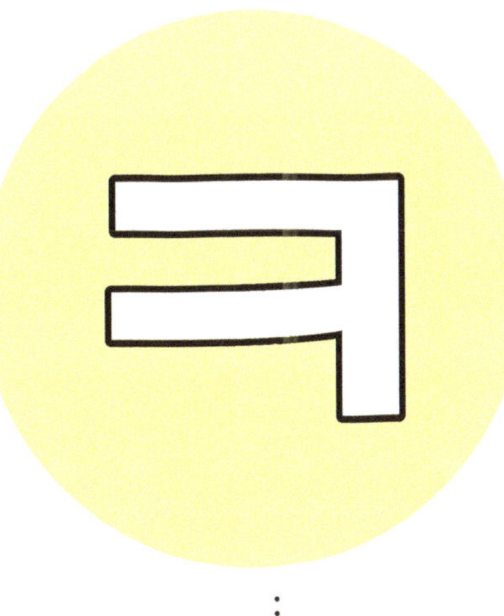

키읔

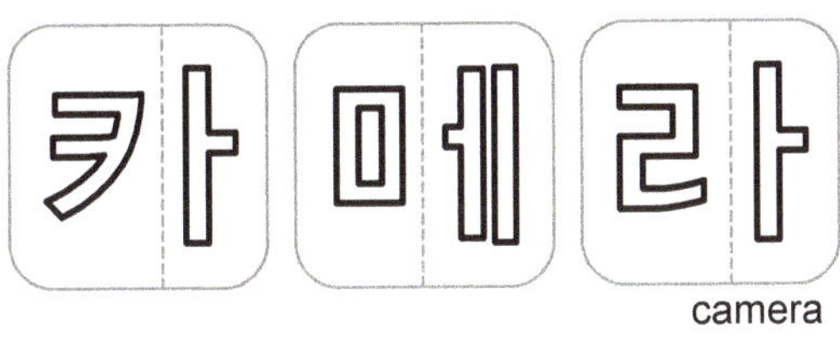

camera

coffee

elephant

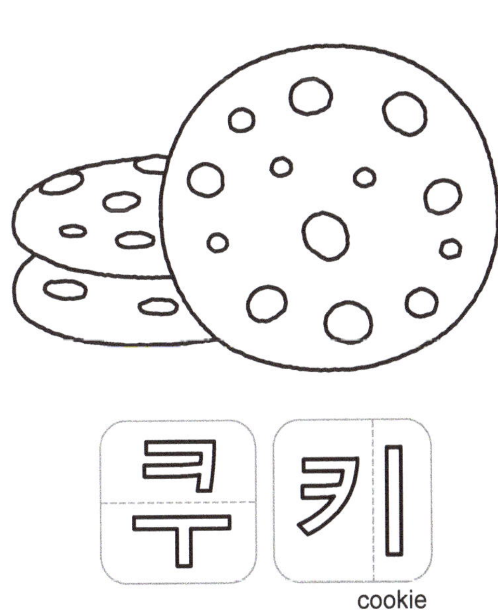

cookie

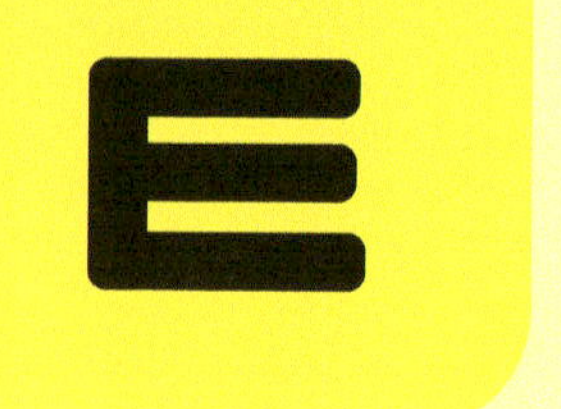

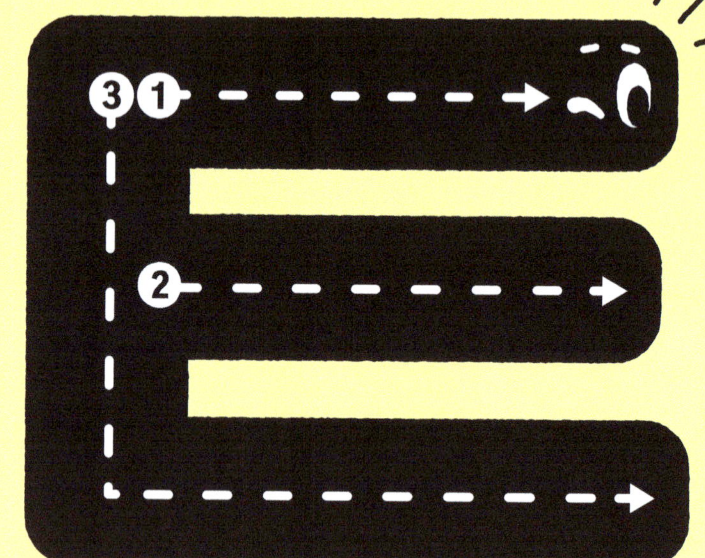

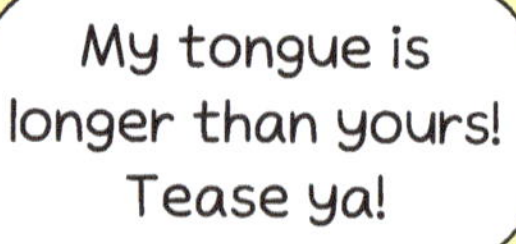

티읕 tieut

sounds [t] of tiger

Let's write together from here.

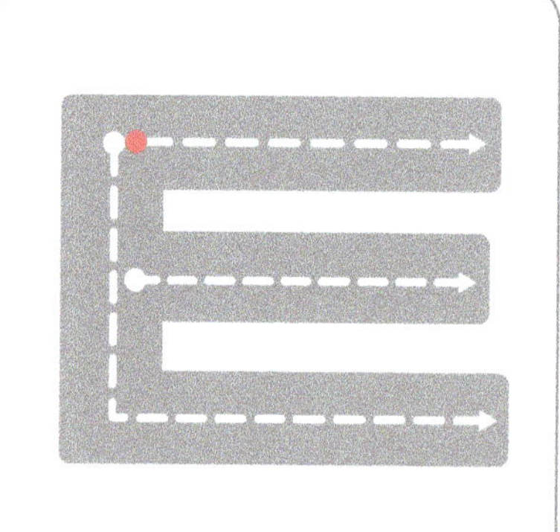

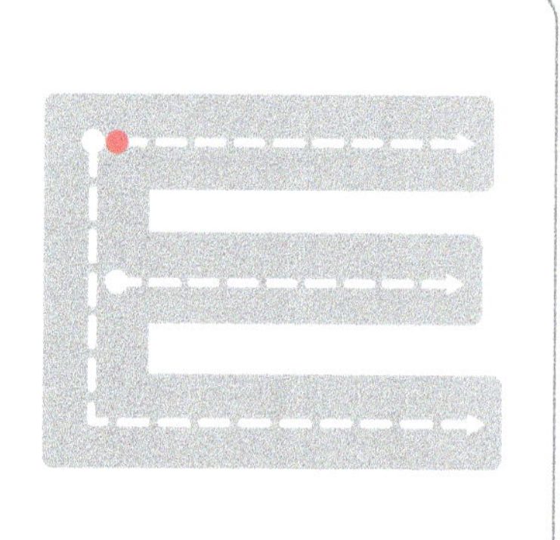

Please start here.

Try writing it yourself.

You're great!

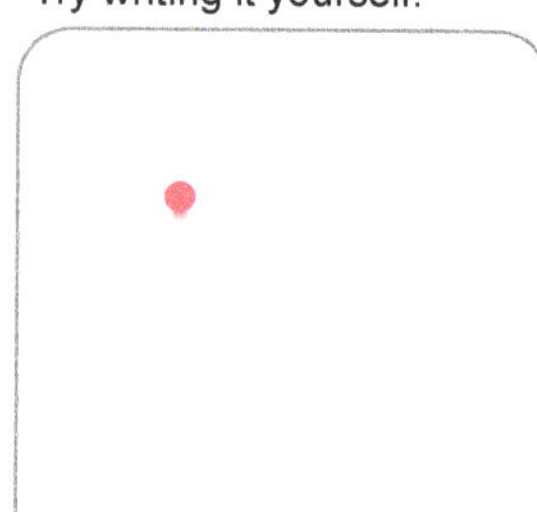

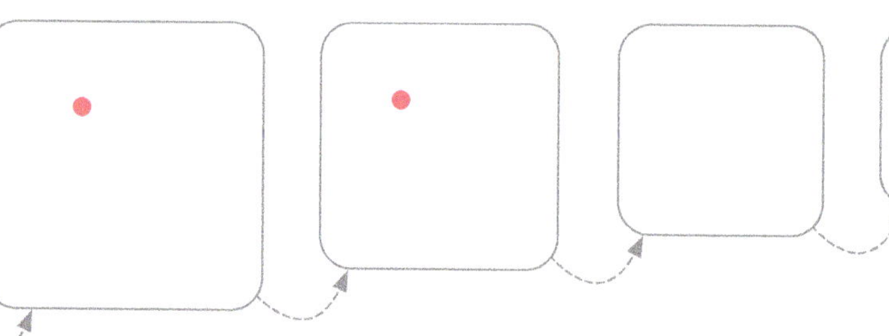

Try challenging yourself with smaller writing.

Here!

Color ㅌ

티읕

티셔츠

T-shirt

타조

ostrich

트럭

truck

토마토

tomato

ㅍ

Try following me.
Stretch your arms to the side and extend your legs to the side as well.

피읖 pieup
sounds [p] of pig

Let's write together from here.

Please start here.

Try writing it yourself.

Fantastic!

Try challenging yourself with smaller writing.

ㄱ ㄴ ㄷ ㄹ ㅁ ㅂ ㅅ ㅇ ㅈ ㅊ ㅋ ㅌ ㅍ ㅎ

Here!

Color ㅍ

ㅍ

피읖

피아노

piano

파도

wave

퍼즐

puzzle

포도

grapes

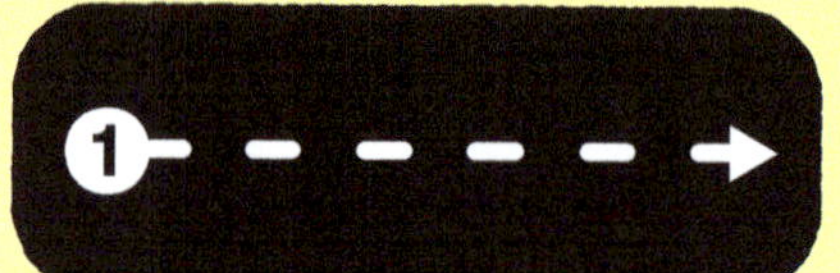

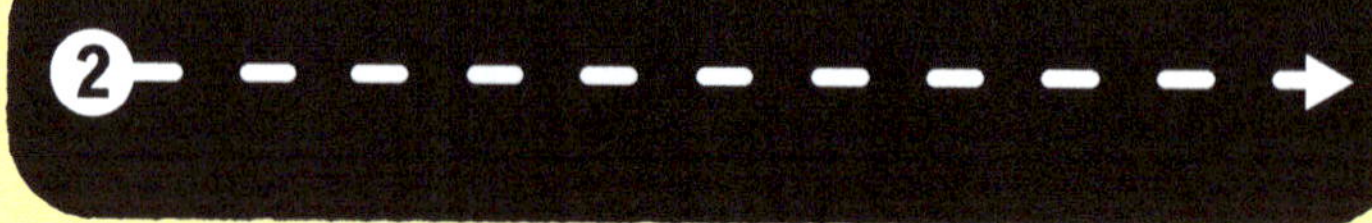

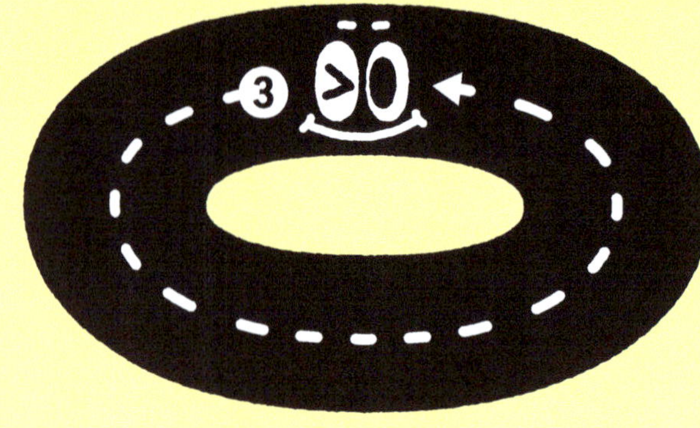

I love wearing hats! I have a lot of hats in my wardrobe. Aren't my hats cool?

히읗 hieut

sounds [h] of hat

Let's write together from here.

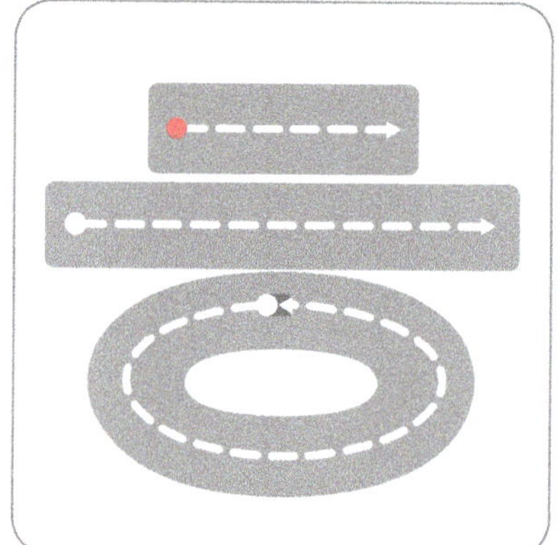

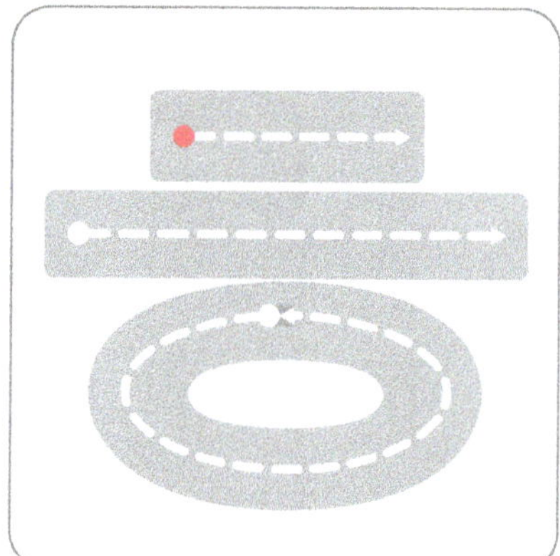

Please start here.

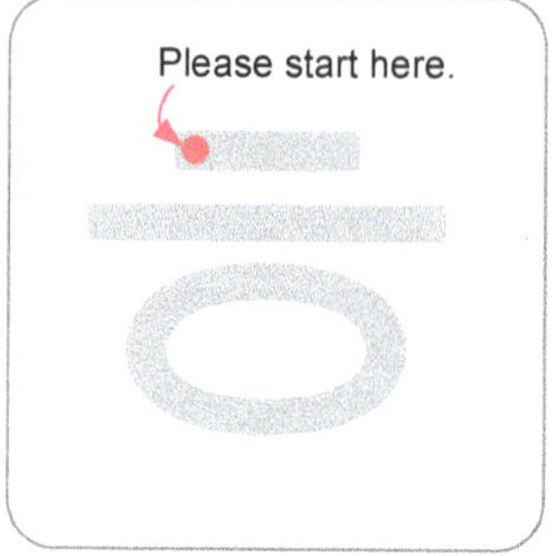

Try writing it yourself.

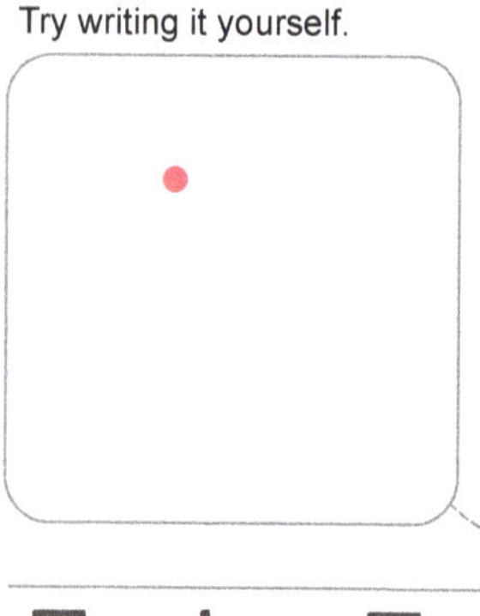

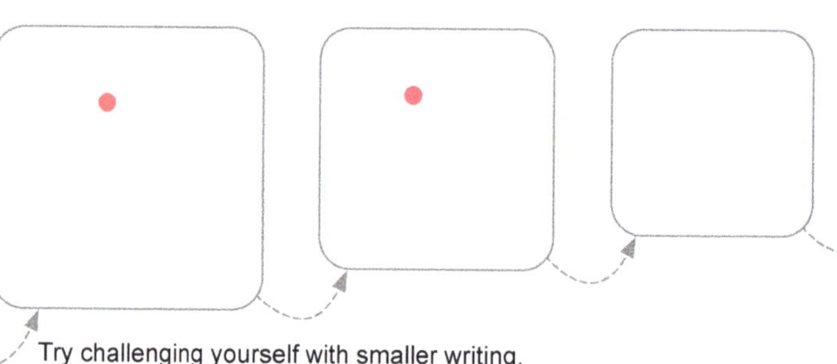

Excellent!

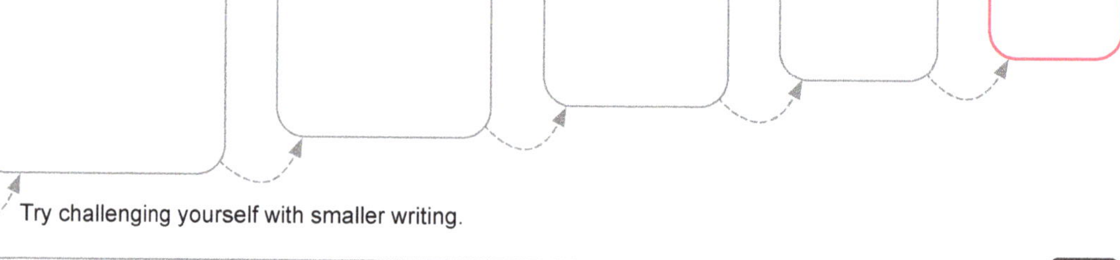

Try challenging yourself with smaller writing.

ㄱ ㄴ ㄷ ㄹ ㅁ ㅂ ㅅ ㅇ ㅈ ㅊ ㅋ ㅌ ㅍ ㅎ

Here!

Color ㅎ

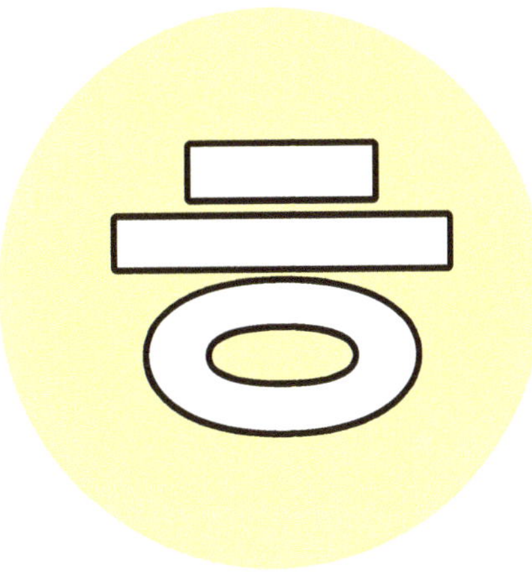

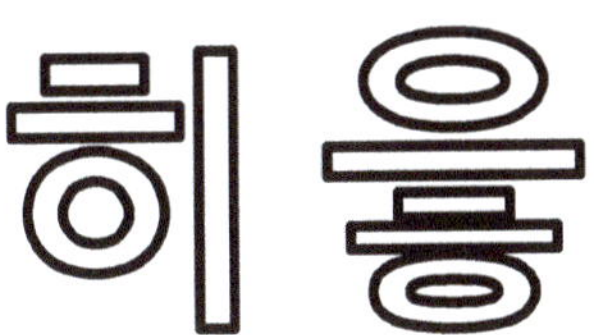

하마

hippopotamus

허리

waist

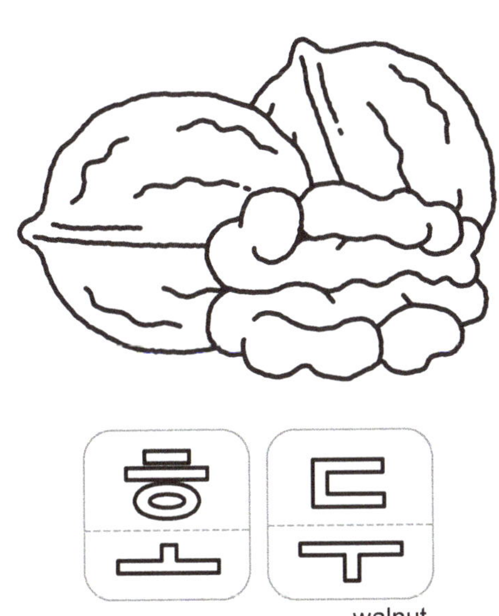

호두

walnut

후추

black pepper

Review

Complete the consonant table by reading and writing consonants in order.

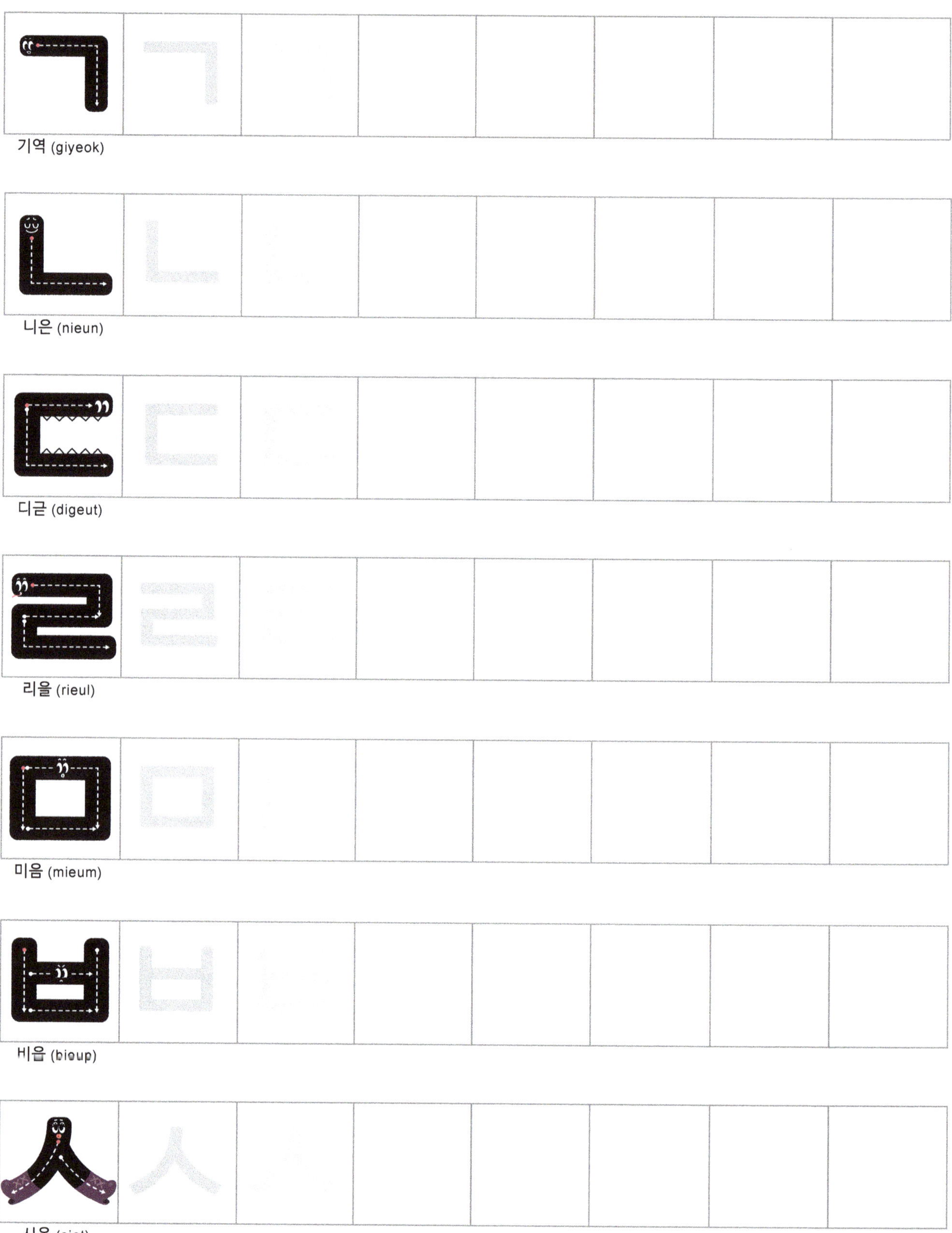

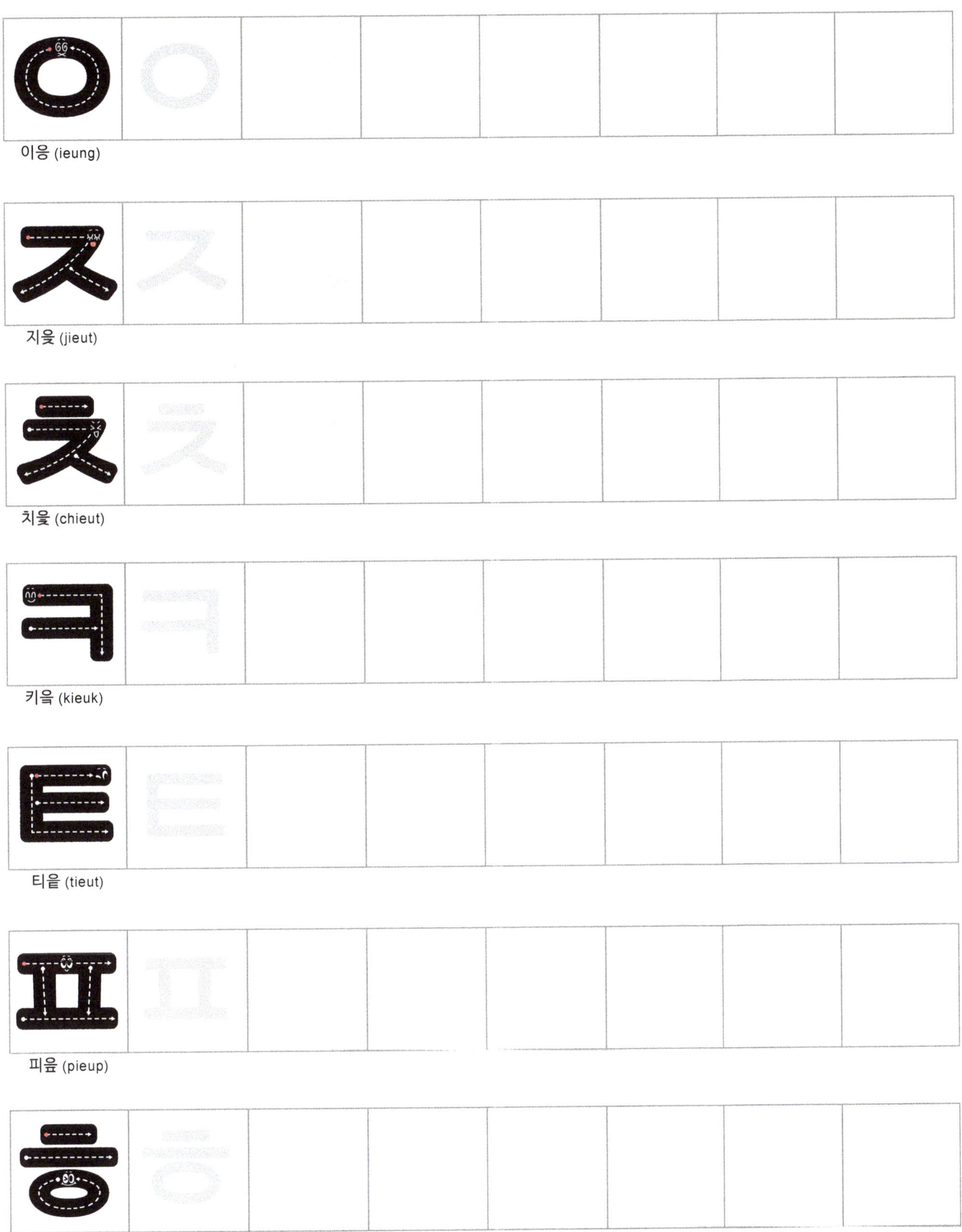
이응 (ieung)
지읒 (jieut)
치읓 (chieut)
키읔 (kieuk)
티읕 (tieut)
피읖 (pieup)
히읗 (hieut)

Special tips

How to distinguish similar-looking consonants.

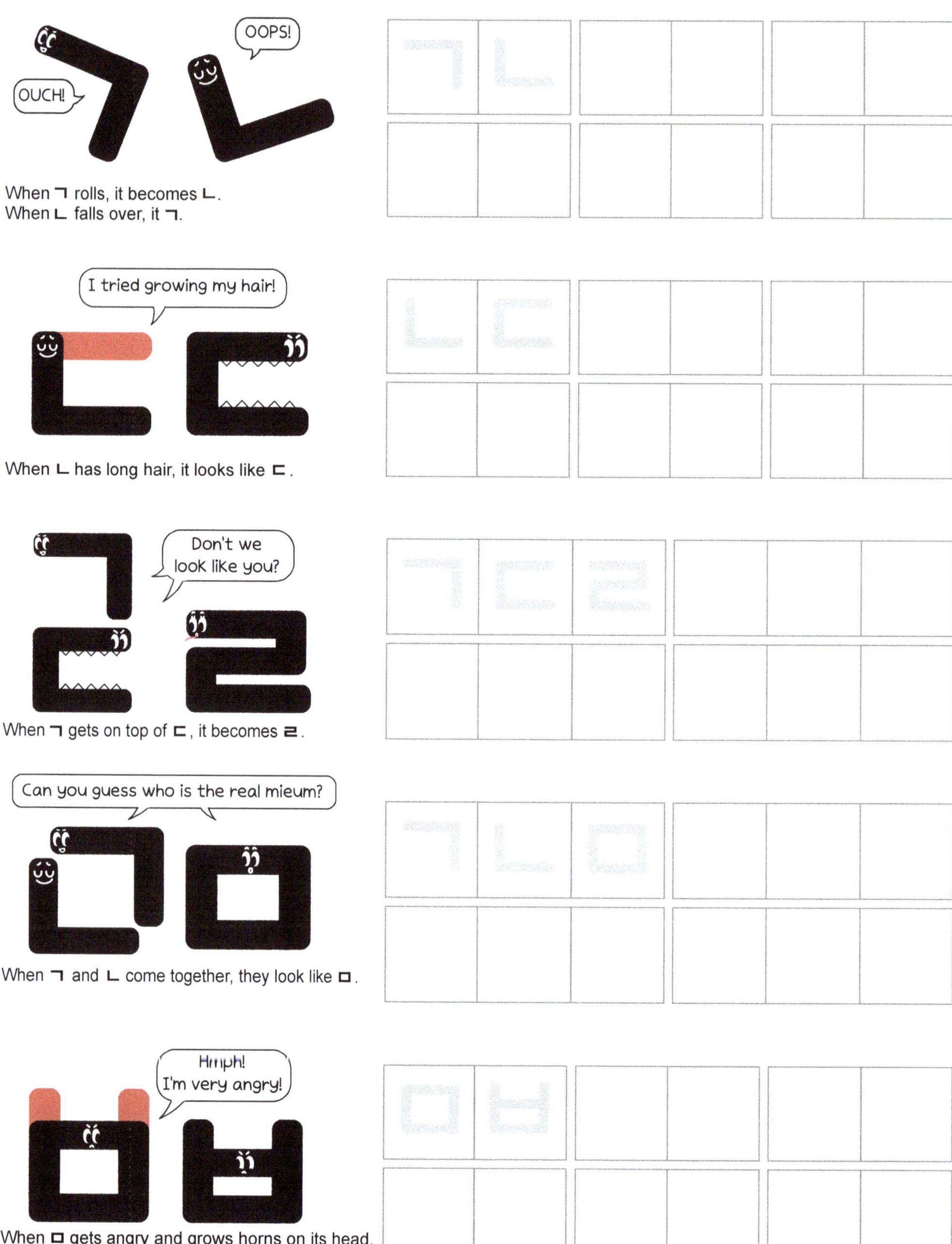

When ㄱ rolls, it becomes ㄴ.
When ㄴ falls over, it ㄱ.

When ㄴ has long hair, it looks like ㄷ.

When ㄱ gets on top of ㄷ, it becomes ㄹ.

When ㄱ and ㄴ come together, they look like ㅁ.

When ㅁ gets angry and grows horns on its head, it looks like ㅂ.

Learning Consonant Special Tips Video

Look at my luscious hair!

When ㅅ has long hair, it looks like ㅈ.

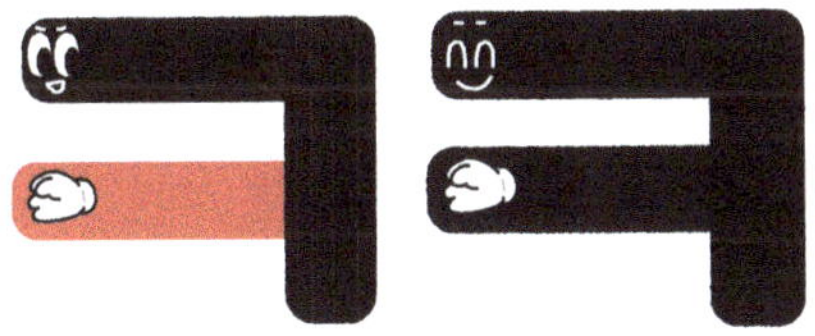

When ㄱ reaches out its hand for a handshake, it looks like ㅋ.

Tease ya!

When ㄷ sticks out its tongue, it looks like ㅌ.

Stretch out your arms and legs wide!

When ㅁ stretches out its arms and legs, it looks like ㅍ.

My hat is just as stylish, isn't it?

When ㅇ wears a hat, it looks like ㅎ.

Chapter2

Vowels

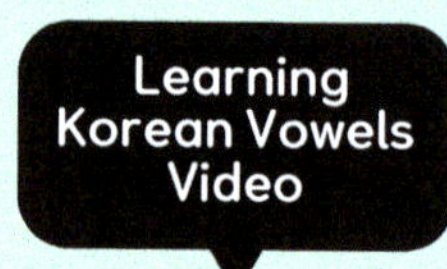

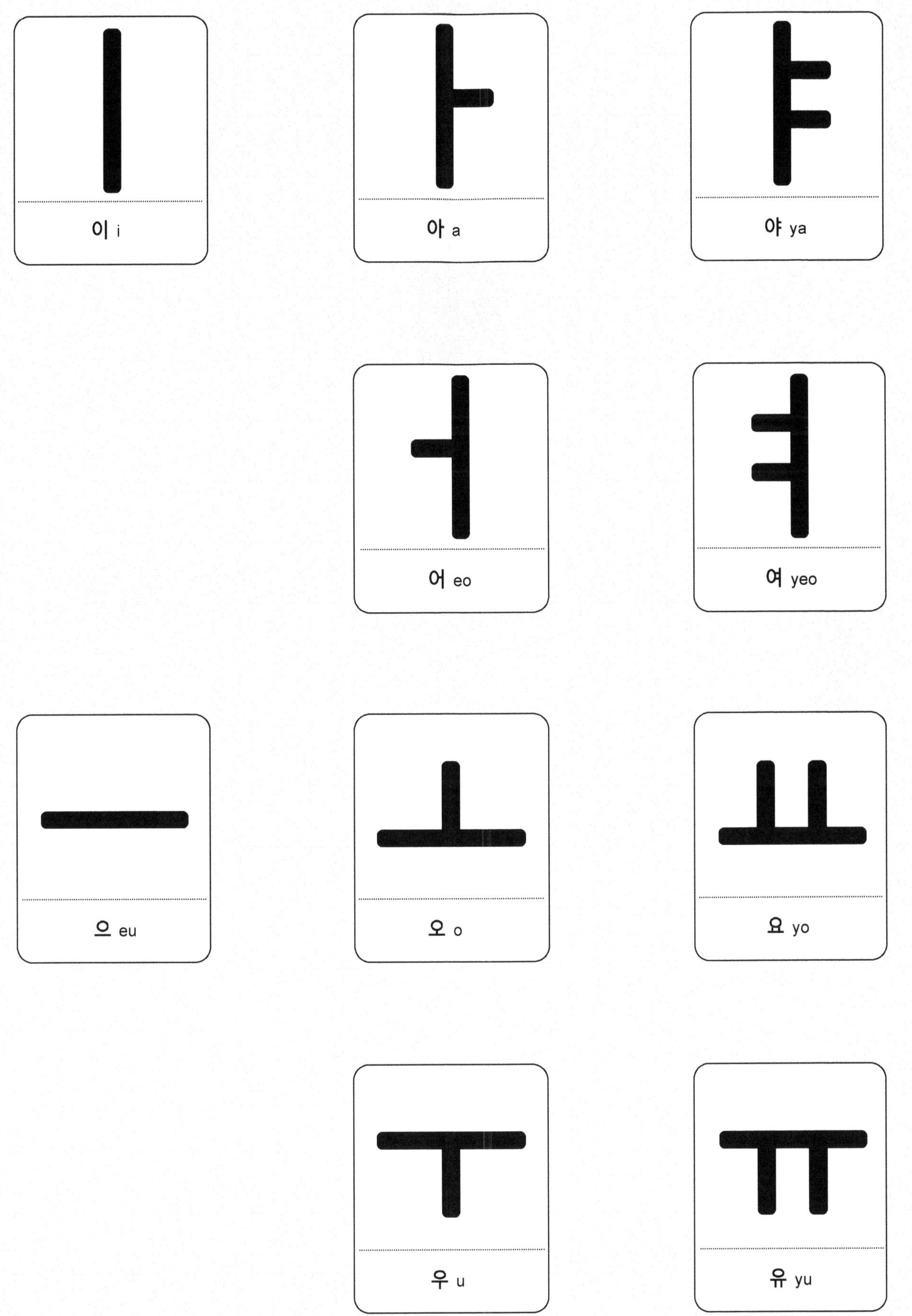
이 i
아 a
야 ya
어 eo
여 yeo
으 eu
오 o
요 yo
우 u
유 yu

ㅣ

이 i

sounds [i] of igloo

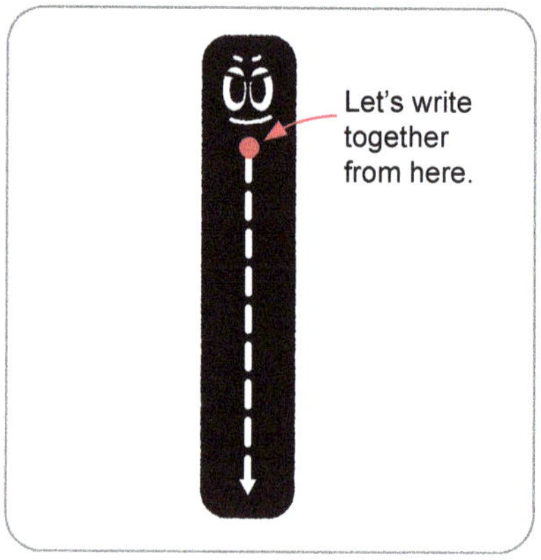

Let's write together from here.

Please start here.

Try writing it yourself.

Well done!

Try challenging yourself with smaller writing.

ㅣ ㅏ ㅑ ㅓ ㅕ ㅡ ㅗ ㅛ ㅜ ㅠ

Here!

Color ㅣ

ㅣ

이

이

tooth

이야기

story

이름

name

이불

blanket

ㅏ

Thank you
for the gift!
1
2

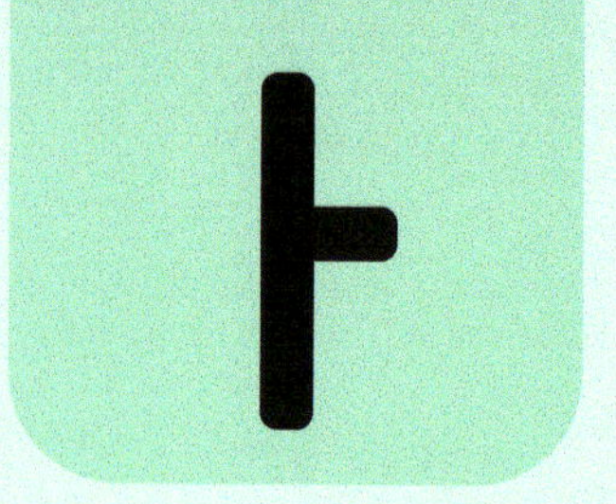

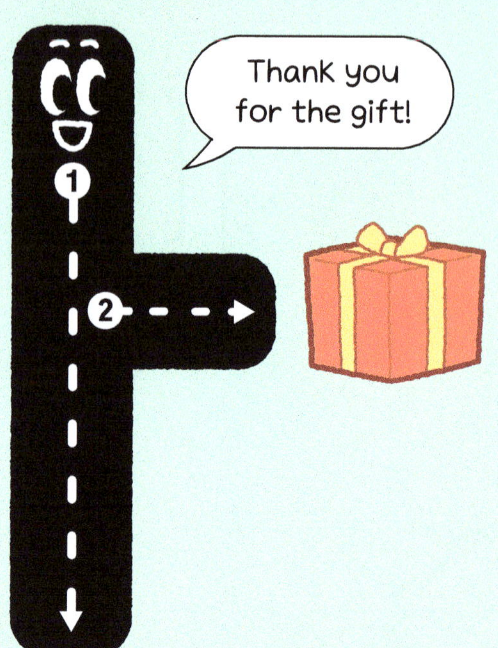

아 a

sounds [a] of apartment

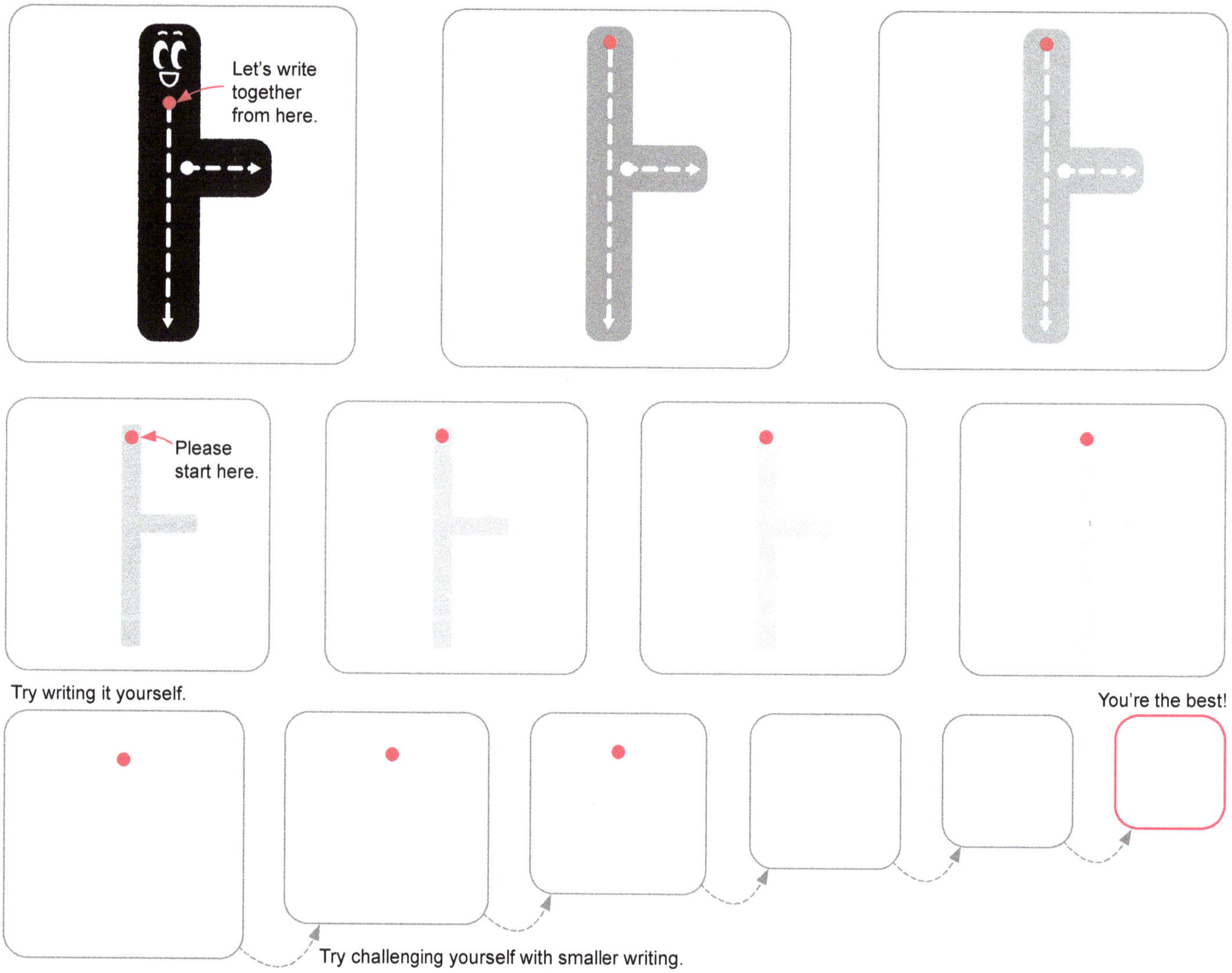
Let's write
together
from here.
Please
start here.
Try writing it yourself.
You're the best!
Try challenging yourself with smaller writing.

ㅣ ㅏ ㅑ ㅓ ㅕ ㅡ ㅗ ㅛ ㅜ ㅠ

Here!

Color ㅏ

ㅏ

아

아파트

apartment

아빠

dad

아몬드

almond

아이스크림

ice cream

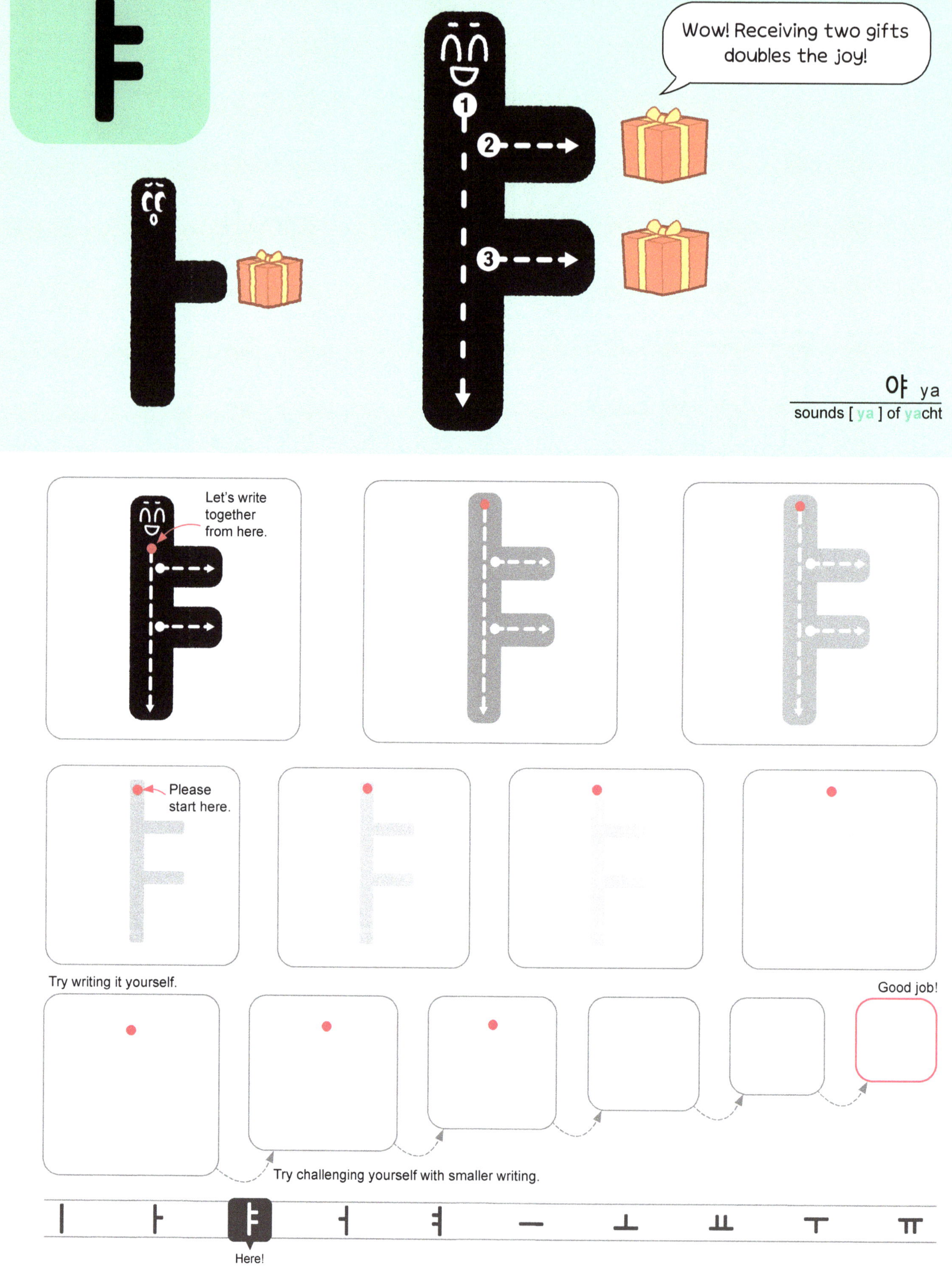
ㅑ
Wow! Receiving two gifts doubles the joy!
1
2
3
야 ya
sounds [ya] of yacht
Let's write together from here.
Please start here.
Try writing it yourself.
Good job!
Try challenging yourself with smaller writing.
ㅣ ㅏ ㅑ ㅓ ㅕ ㅡ ㅗ ㅛ ㅜ ㅠ
Here!

Color ㅑ

ㅑ

야

야 구

baseball

야 자 수

palm tree

야 호

hooray

야 채

vegetable

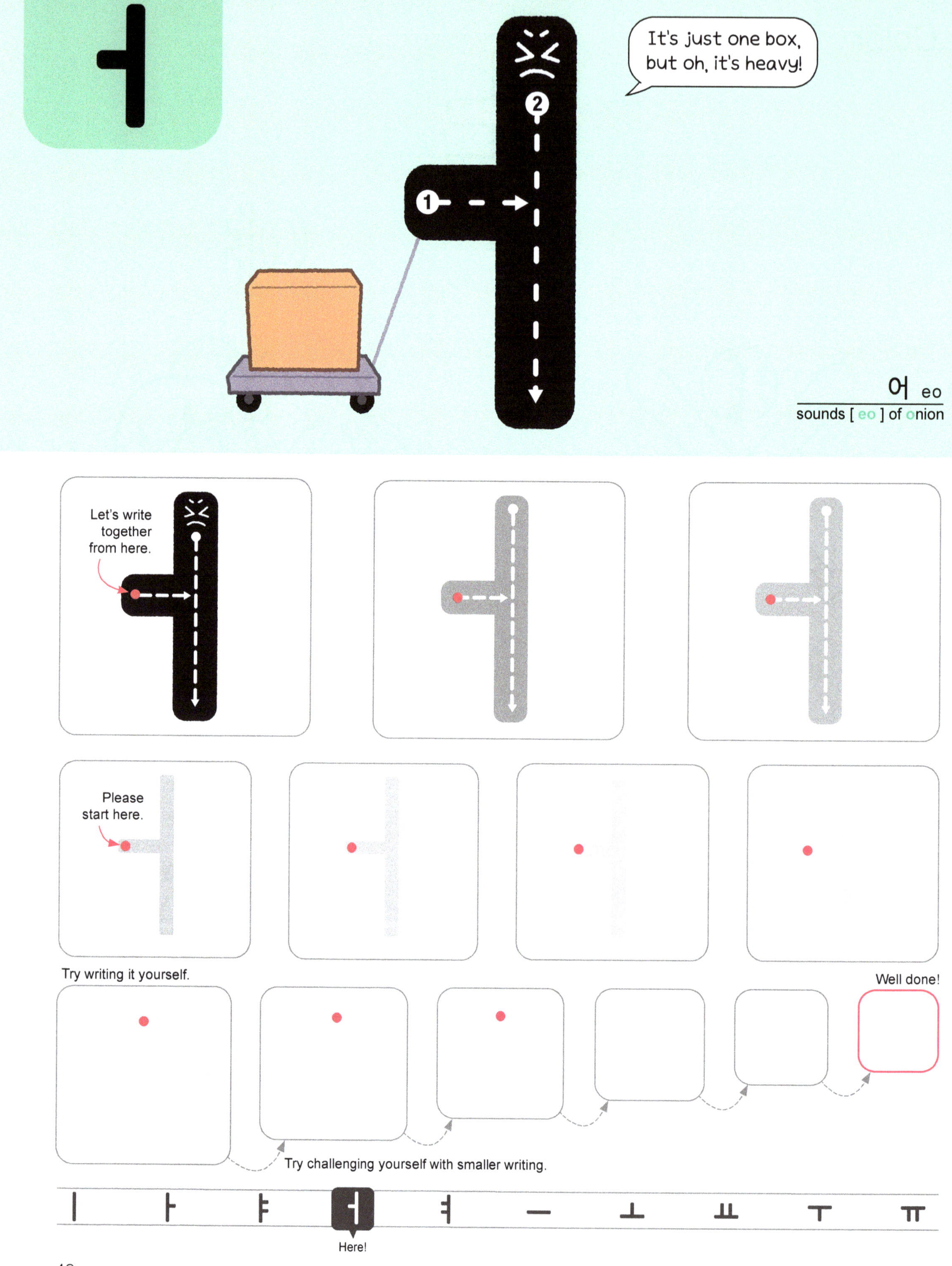
ㅓ
It's just one box,
but oh, it's heavy!
어 eo
sounds [eo] of onion
Let's write together from here.
Please start here.
Try writing it yourself.
Well done!
Try challenging yourself with smaller writing.
ㅣ ㅏ ㅑ ㅓ ㅕ ㅡ ㅗ ㅛ ㅜ ㅠ
Here!

Color ㅓ

ㅓ

어

어부

fisherman

어깨

shoulder

어항

fish bowl

엄마

mom

ㅕ

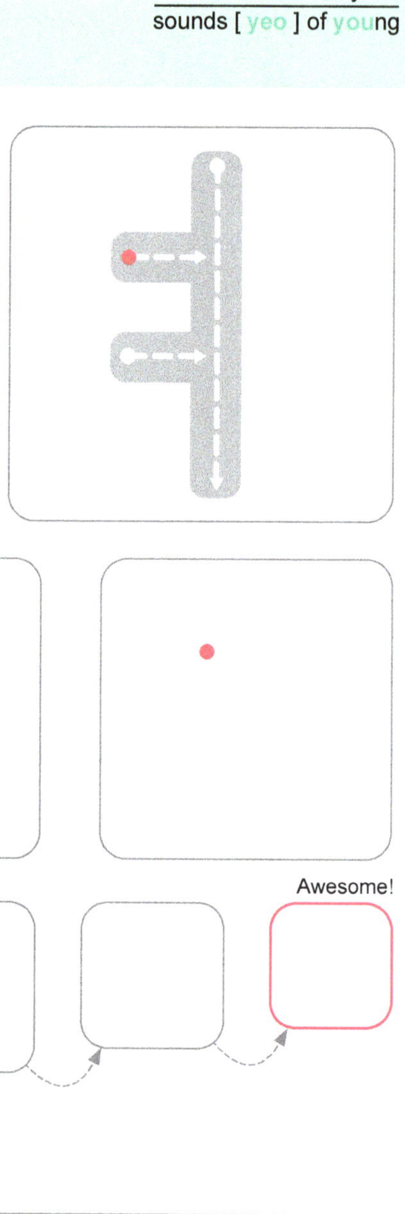

여 yeo

sounds [yeo] of young

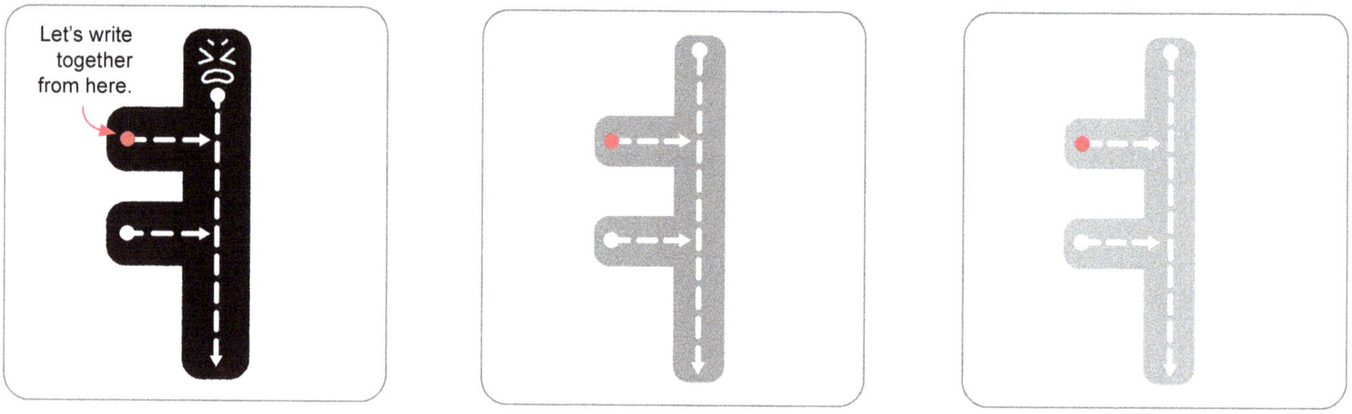

Let's write together from here.

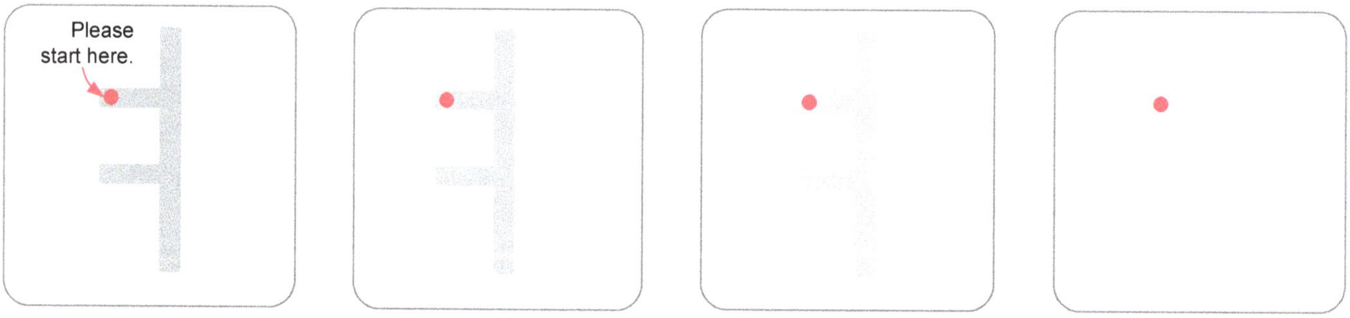

Please start here.

Try writing it yourself.

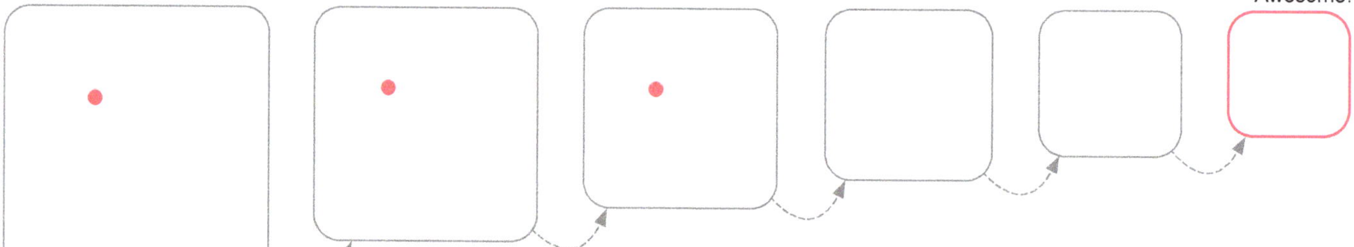

Try challenging yourself with smaller writing.

Awesome!

ㅣ ㅏ ㅑ ㅓ ㅕ ㅡ ㅗ ㅛ ㅜ ㅠ

Here!

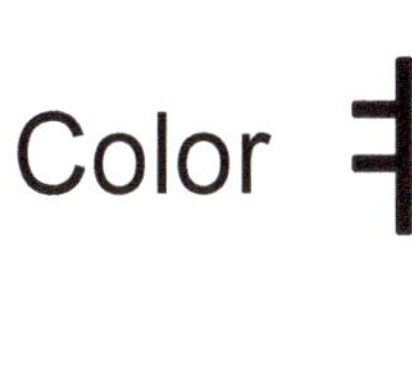

Color ㅕ

ㅕ

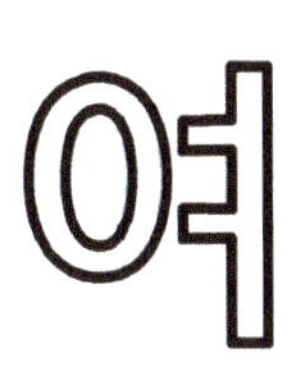

여

여우

fox

여보세요

hello

여름

summer

여섯

six

ㅡ

ㅡ eu

sounds [eu] of taken

Let's write together from here.

Please start here.

Try writing it yourself.

Good job!

Try challenging yourself with smaller writing.

ㅣ ㅏ ㅑ ㅓ ㅕ ㅡ ㅗ ㅛ ㅜ ㅠ

Here!

Color ㅡ

ㅡ

으

으깨다

mash

으르렁

growl

으쓱이다

shrug

으슬으슬

shiver

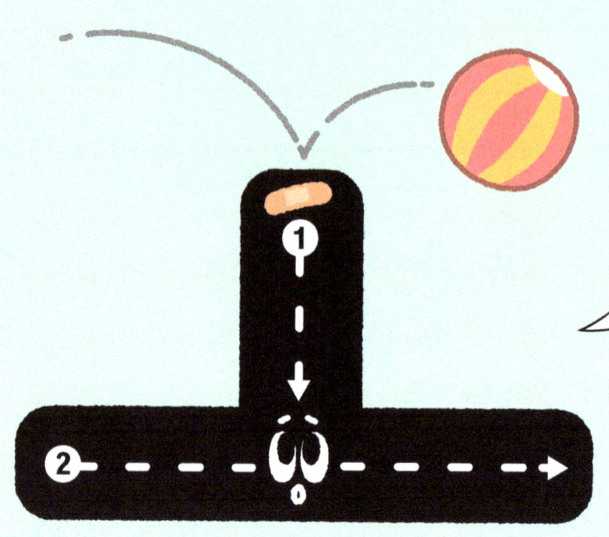

Ouch!
I just got hit by the ball,
and I got a bump
on my head!

오 o

sounds [o] of orange

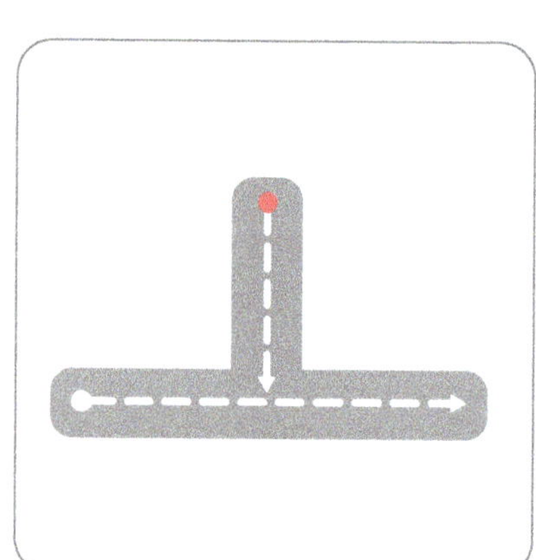

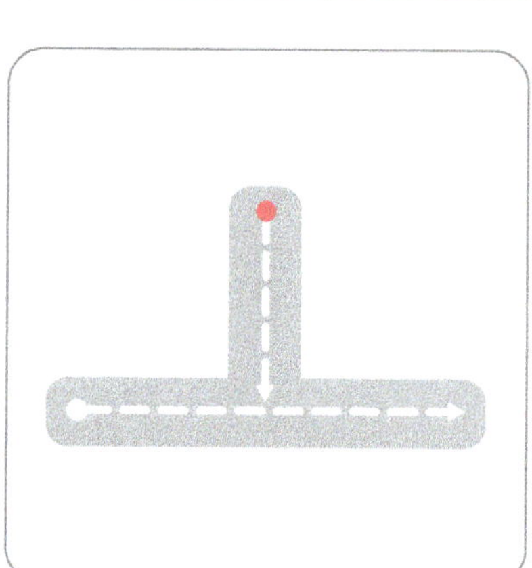

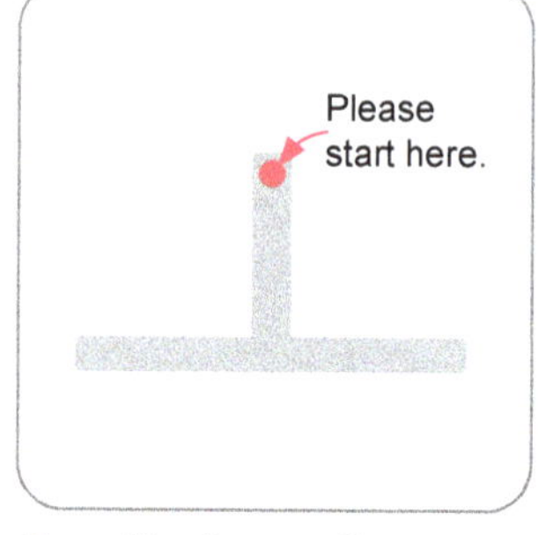

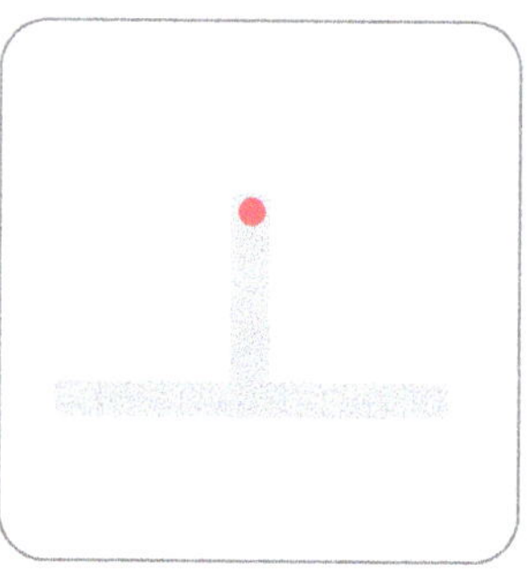

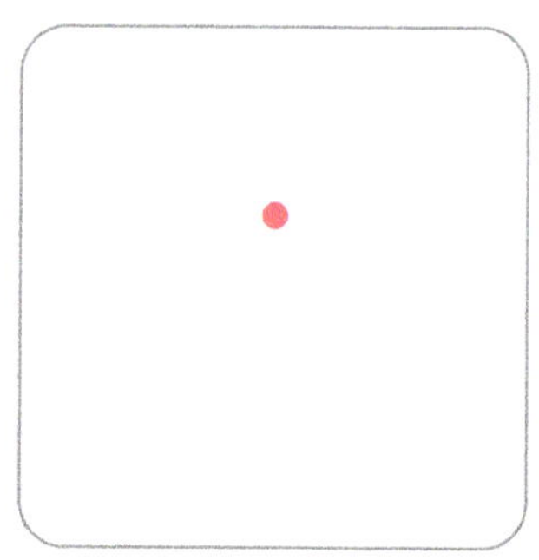

Try writing it yourself.

You're the great!

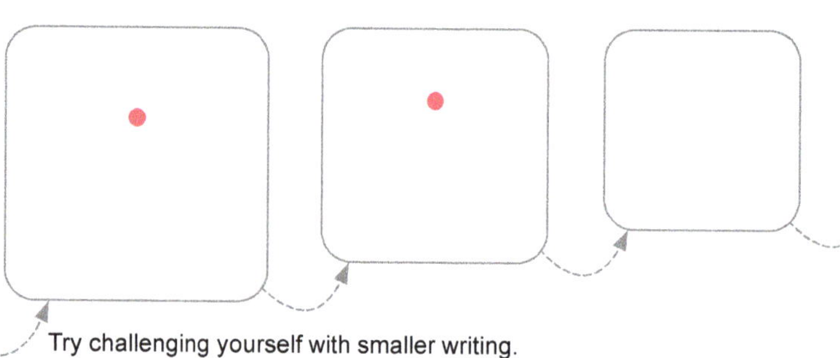

Try challenging yourself with smaller writing.

ㅣ ㅏ ㅑ ㅓ ㅕ ㅡ ㅗ ㅛ ㅜ ㅠ

Here!

Color ㅗ

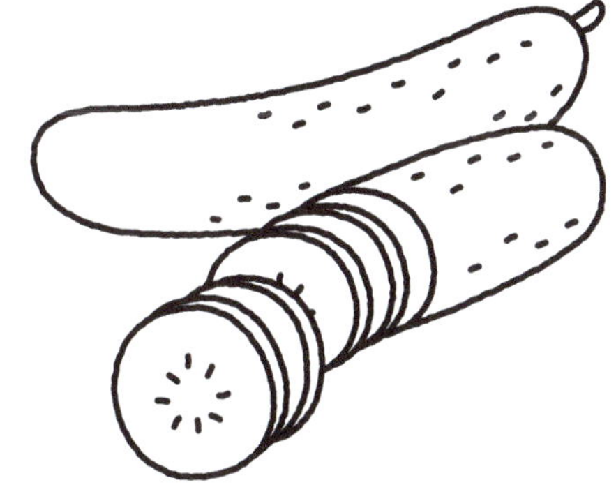

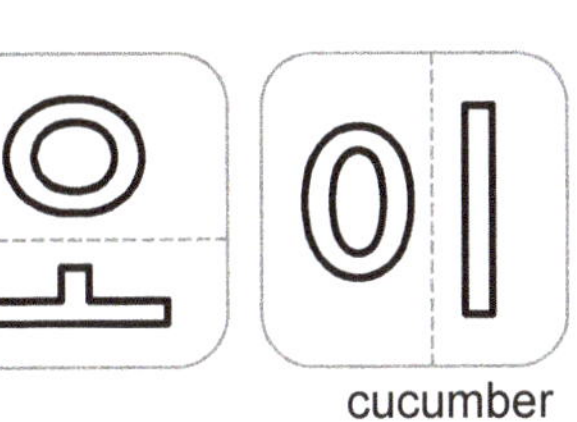

cucumber

오토바이

motorcycle

squid

orange

Let's write together from here.

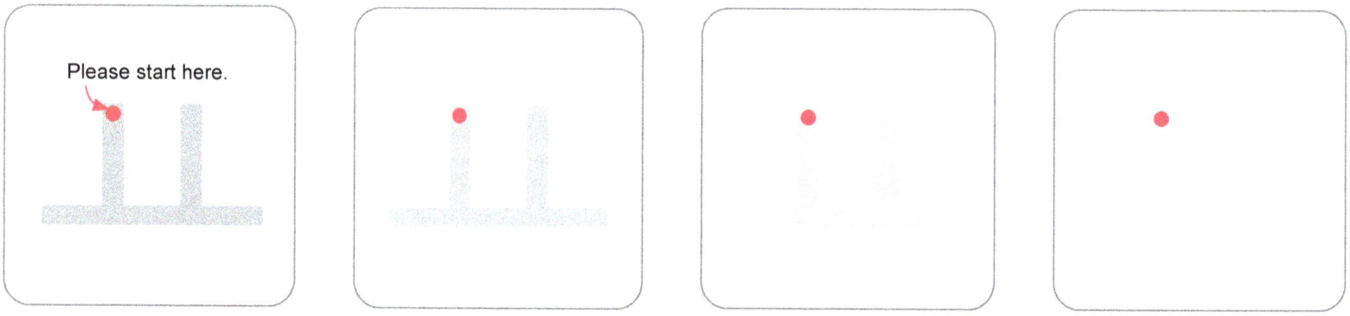

Please start here.

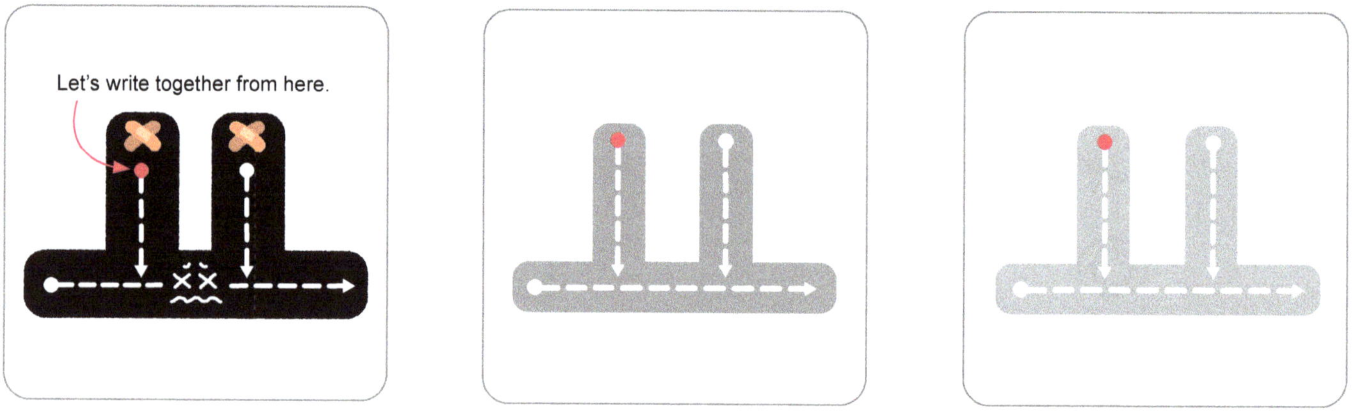

Try writing it yourself.

Fantastic!

Try challenging yourself with smaller writing.

ㅣ ㅏ ㅑ ㅓ ㅕ ㅡ ㅗ ㅛ ㅜ ㅠ

Here!

Color ㅛ

요

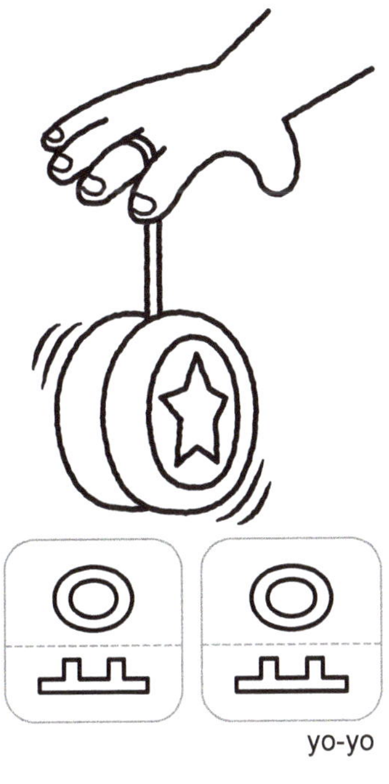

요요

yo-yo

요리사

cook

요트

yacht

요정

fairy

ㅜ

우 u

sounds [u] of soup

Let's write together from here.

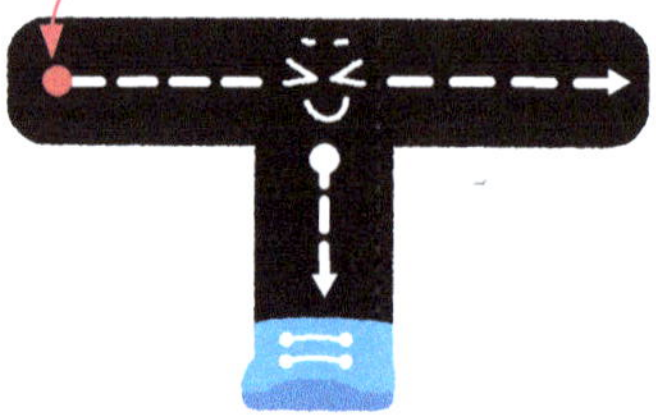

Please start here.

Try writing it yourself.

Excellent!

Try challenging yourself with smaller writing.

ㅣ ㅏ ㅑ ㅓ ㅕ ㅡ ㅗ ㅛ ㅜ ㅠ

Here!

Color ㅜ

ㅜ

우

우비

raincoat

우표

stamp

우산

umbrella

우주선

spaceship

ㅠ

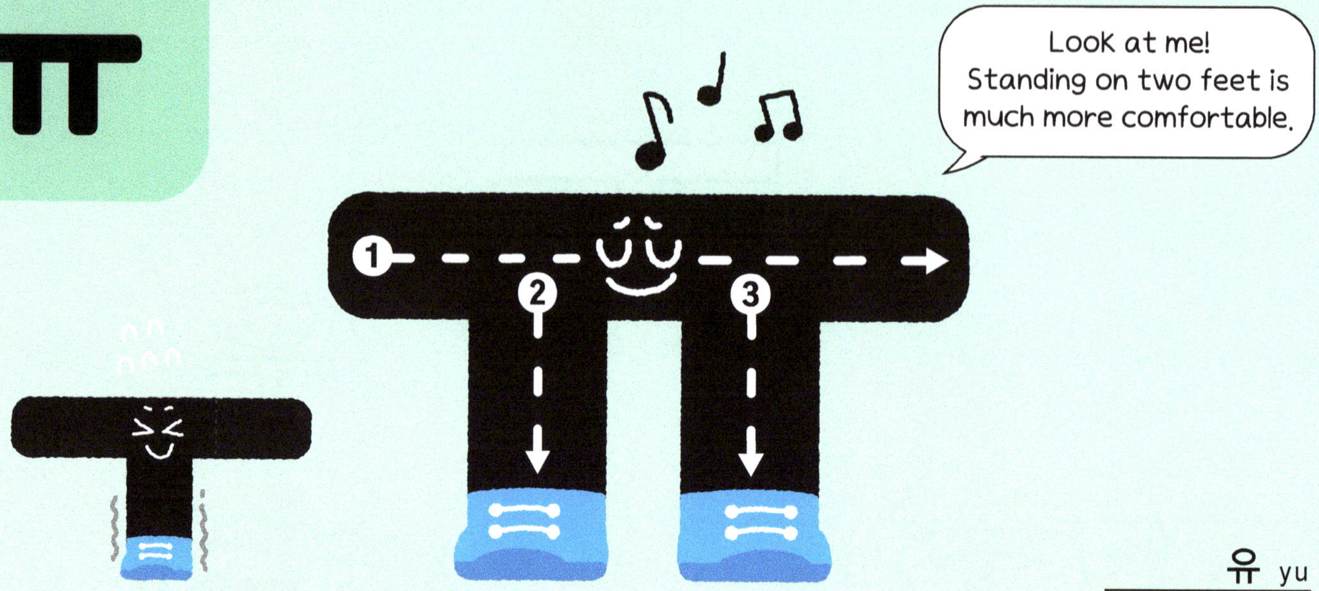

Look at me!
Standing on two feet is much more comfortable.

유 yu

sounds [yu] of you

Let's write together from here.

Please start here.

Try writing it yourself.

You're the best!

Try challenging yourself with smaller writing.

ㅣ ㅏ ㅑ ㅓ ㅕ ㅡ ㅗ ㅛ ㅜ ㅠ

Here!

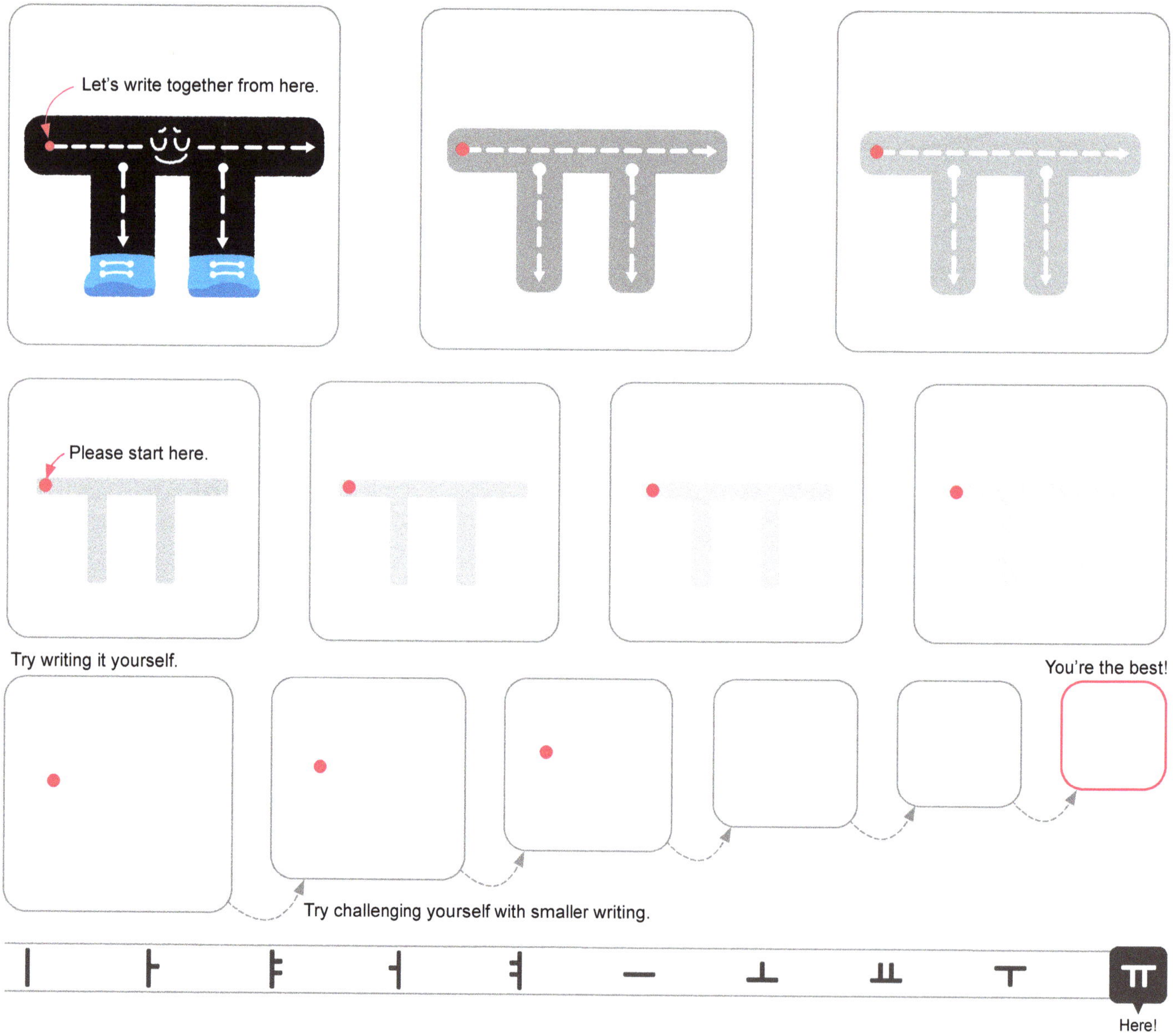

Color ㅠ

ㅠ

유

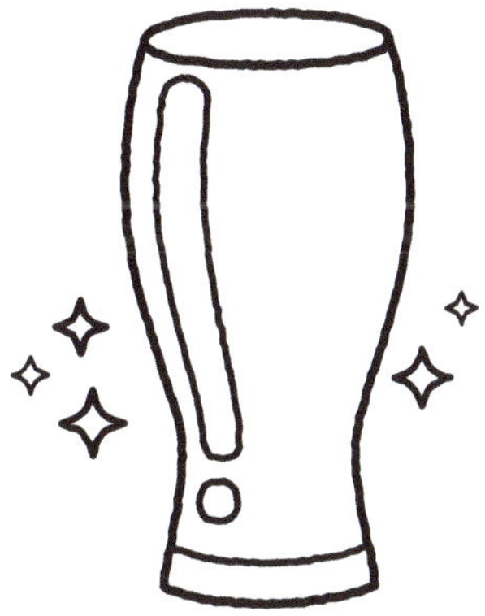

유리

glass

유아차

stroller

유령

ghost

유럽

Europe

Review

Complete the vowel table by reading and writing consonants in order.

이[i]	ㄱ	ㄴ	ㄷ	ㄹ	ㅁ	ㅂ	ㅅ
	ㅇ	ㅈ	ㅊ	ㅋ	ㅌ	ㅍ	ㅎ

아[a]	ㄱ	ㄴ	ㄷ	ㄹ	ㅁ	ㅂ	ㅅ
	ㅇ	ㅈ	ㅊ	ㅋ	ㅌ	ㅍ	ㅎ

야[ya]	ㄱ	ㄴ	ㄷ	ㄹ	ㅁ	ㅂ	ㅅ
	ㅇ	ㅈ	ㅊ	ㅋ	ㅌ	ㅍ	ㅎ

어[eo]	ㄱ	ㄴ	ㄷ	ㄹ	ㅁ	ㅂ	ㅅ
	ㅇ	ㅈ	ㅊ	ㅋ	ㅌ	ㅍ	ㅎ

여[yeo]	ㄱ	ㄴ	ㄷ	ㄹ	ㅁ	ㅂ	ㅅ
	ㅇ	ㅈ	ㅊ	ㅋ	ㅌ	ㅍ	ㅎ

ㄱ ㄴ ㄷ ㄹ ㅁ ㅂ ㅅ
ㅇ ㅈ ㅊ ㅋ ㅌ ㅍ ㅎ
으[eu]
ㄱ ㄴ ㄷ ㄹ ㅁ ㅂ ㅅ
ㅇ ㅈ ㅊ ㅋ ㅌ ㅍ ㅎ
오[o]
ㄱ ㄴ ㄷ ㄹ ㅁ ㅂ ㅅ
ㅇ ㅈ ㅊ ㅋ ㅌ ㅍ ㅎ
요[yo]
ㄱ ㄴ ㄷ ㄹ ㅁ ㅂ ㅅ
ㅇ ㅈ ㅊ ㅋ ㅌ ㅍ ㅎ
우[u]
ㄱ ㄴ ㄷ ㄹ ㅁ ㅂ ㅅ
ㅇ ㅈ ㅊ ㅋ ㅌ ㅍ ㅎ
유[yu]

Special tips

Vowels are composed of long and short lines.
Comparing the positions of the short lines makes it easy to remember vowels.

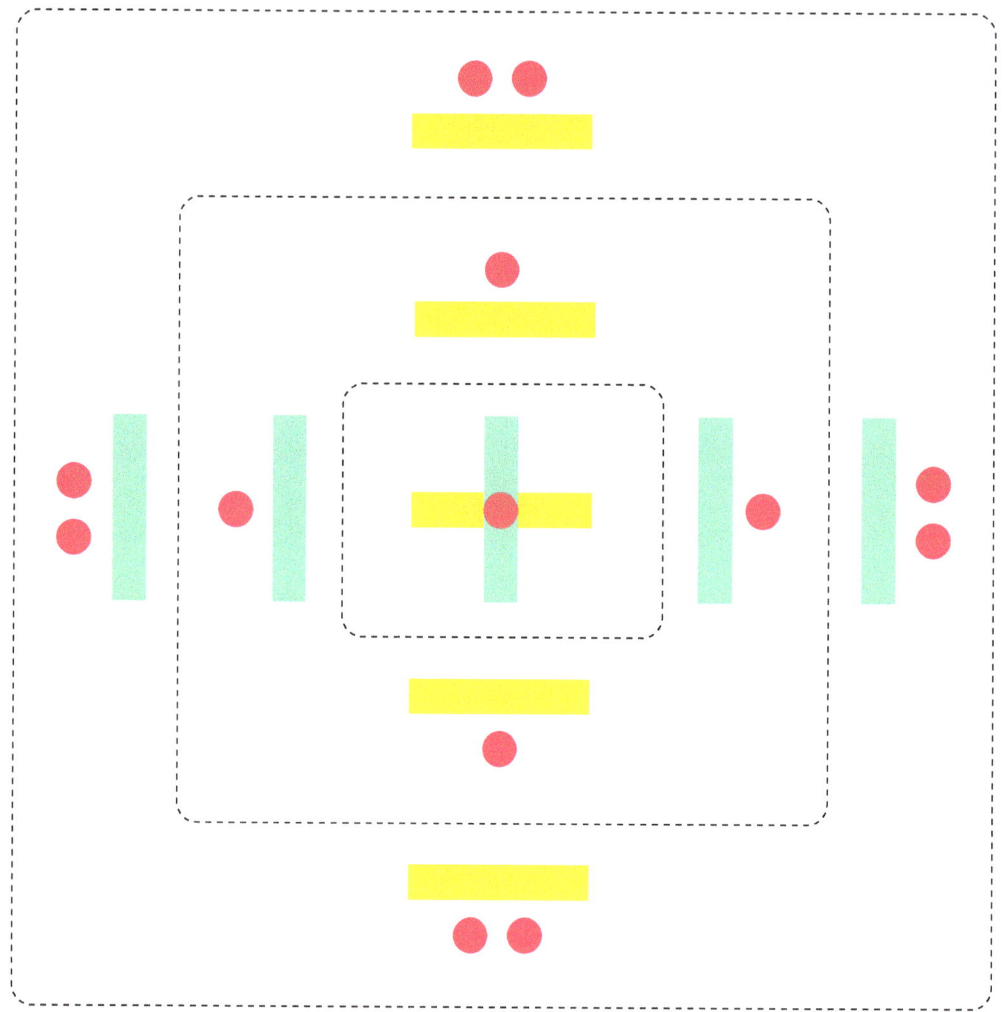

Vowels are created based on the fundamental elements, 천지인 Cheonjiin, representing heaven, earth, and mankind (• ― |).
Knowing these three elements makes it easy to create vowels.
The dot (•) representing heaven is expressed with a short line today.

When the line representing mankind (|) meets the dot (•) representing heaven, you can create characters like ㅏ, ㅑ, ㅓ, ㅕ depending on the direction of the meeting point.
Similarly, when the line representing the earth (―) meets the dot (•) representing heaven, you can create characters like ㅗ, ㅛ, ㅜ, ㅠ.

Understanding the spatial characteristics of vowel helps you grasp the vowels in a three-dimensional way, making it easier for beginners to learn.

Easy ways to remember vowels.

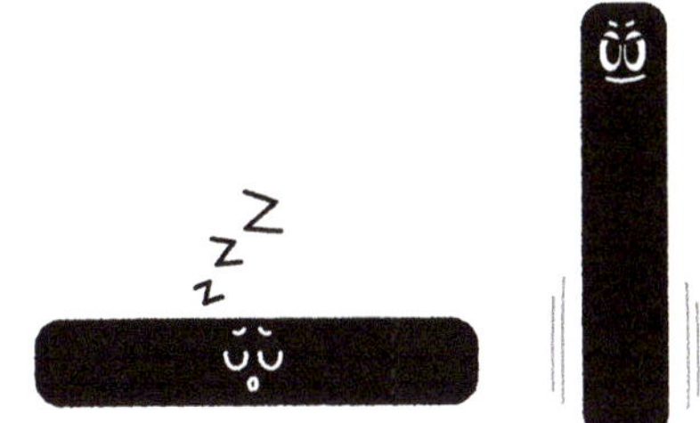

Either standing up or lying down.

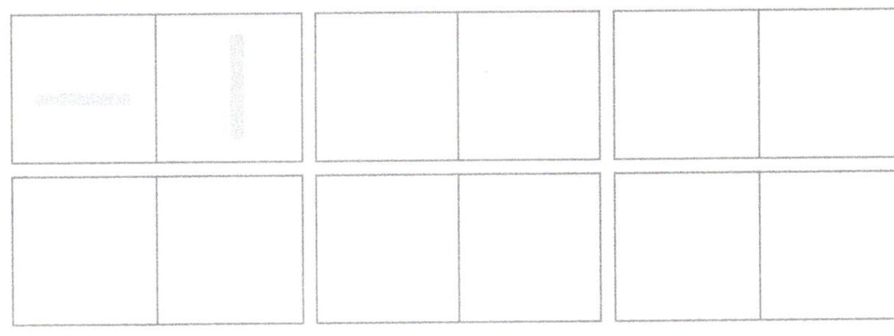

Either receiving one gift or two gifts.

Either dragging one box or two boxes.

Either having one bump or two bumps.

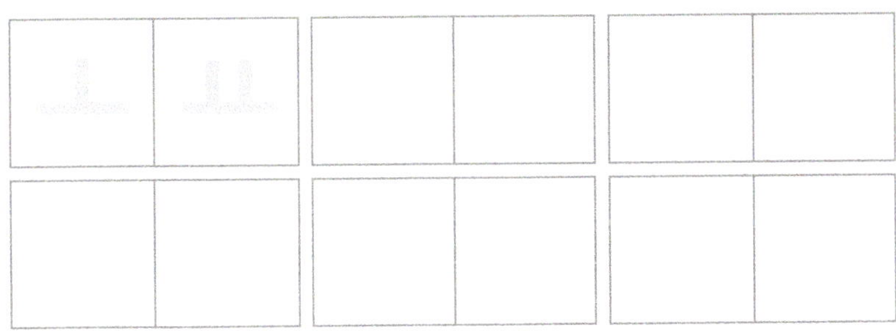

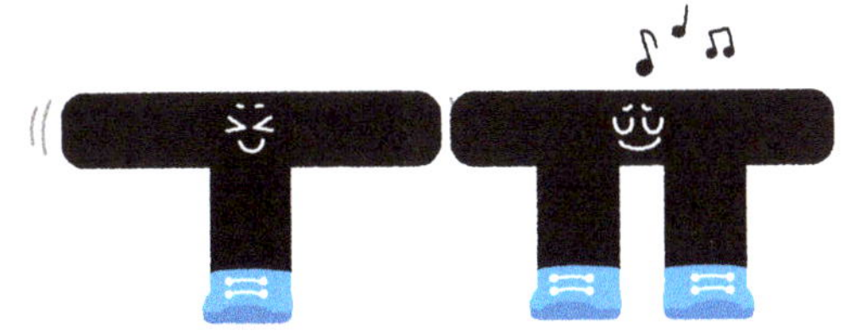

Either standing on one foot or two feet.

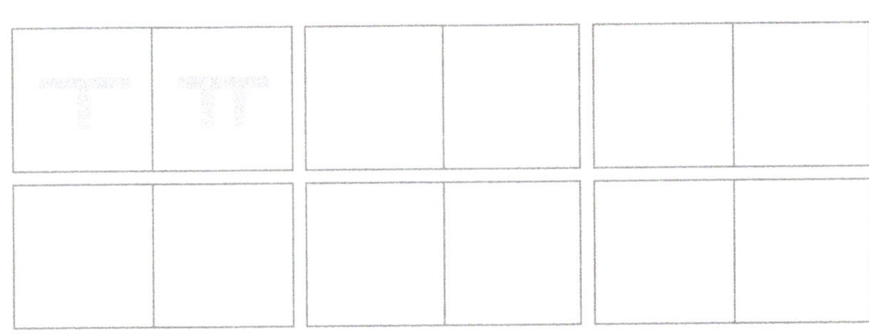

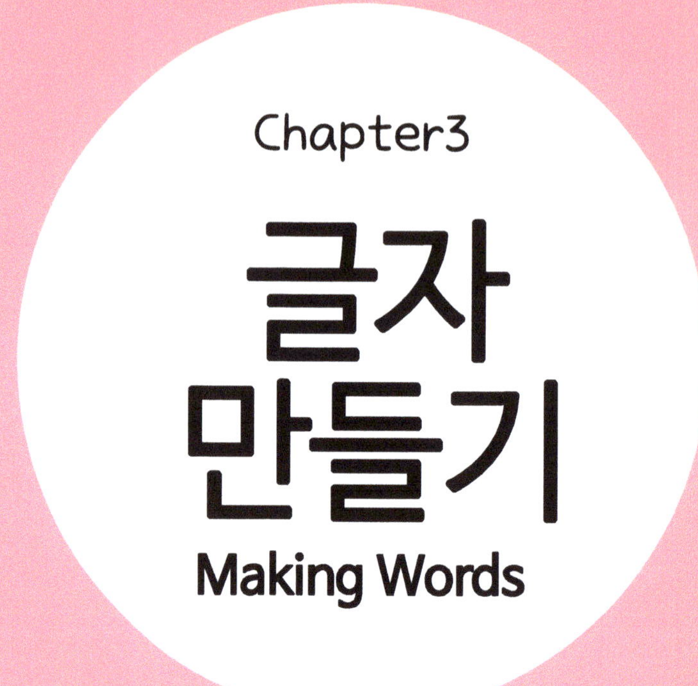

Chapter3

글자 만들기

Making Words

Make words by combining consonants and vowels.

To create a Korean word, at least one vowel and one consonant are required. Consonants and vowels combine to form syllable blocks, which then create words. Syllable blocks can be combined in various ways, but in this workbook, we will explore the most basic horizontal and vertical combinations of consonants and vowels.

Vertical Combination

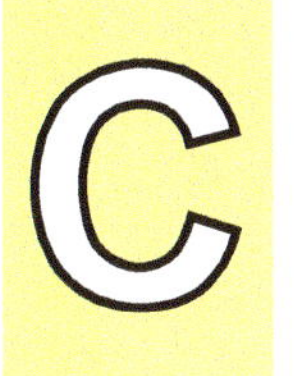

Consonants are positioned on the left, and vowels on the right.
This arrangement is determined by the type of vowel used.
Vowels that combine vertically include ㅣ, ㅏ, ㅑ, ㅓ, ㅕ.

By bringing the blocks a little closer, you can create characters with a more refined appearance.

Horizontal Combination

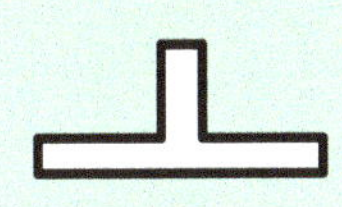

Consonants are positioned at the top, and vowels at the bottom.
The vowels used in this arrangement are ㅡ,ㅗ,ㅛ,ㅜ,ㅠ.

Useful Tip!

The shape of the consonant may vary slightly depending on where the vowel is positioned.
In vertical combination, the shape elongates depending on the vowel positioned on the right.
In horizontal combination, the shape compresses depending on the vowel positioned at the bottom.
Keep practicing while paying attention to the shapes of the consonants, which change depending on where the vowels are positioned.

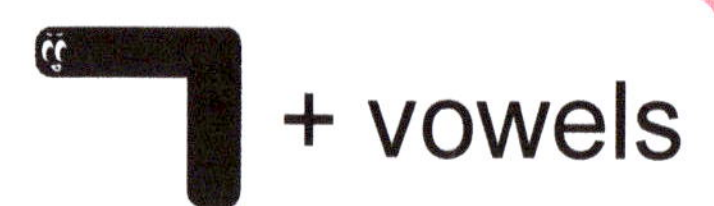

ㄱ + vowels

Write combinations of the consonant 'ㄱ' with vowels.

ㄱ [g] ㅣ [i] = 기 [gi]

ㄱ [g] ㅏ [a] = 가 [ga]

ㄱ [g] ㅑ [ya] = 갸 [gya]

ㄱ [g] ㅓ [eo] = 거 [geo]

ㄱ [g] ㅕ [yeo] = 겨 [gyeo]

ㄱ [g]
ㅡ [eu]
= 그 [geu]

ㄱ [g]
ㅗ [o]
= 고 [go]

ㄱ [g]
ㅛ [yo]
= 교 [gyo]

ㄱ [g]
ㅜ [u]
= 구 [gu]

ㄱ [g]
ㅠ [yu]
= 규 [gyu]

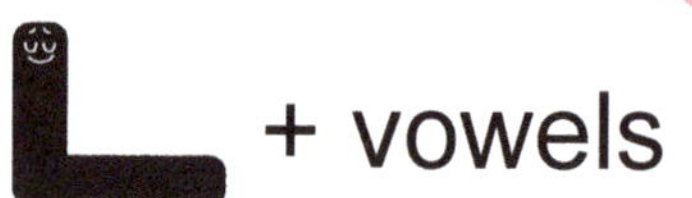

ㄴ + vowels

Write combinations of the consonant 'ㄴ' with vowels.

ㄴ [n] + ㅣ [i] = 니 [ni]

ㄴ [n] + ㅏ [a] = 나 [na]

ㄴ [n] + ㅑ [ya] = 냐 [nya]

ㄴ [n] + ㅓ [eo] = 너 [neo]

ㄴ [n] + ㅕ [yeo] = 녀 [nyeo]

ㄴ [n] + ㅡ [eu] = 느 [neu]

ㄴ [n] + ㅗ [o] = 노 [no]

ㄴ [n] + ㅛ [yo] = 뇨 [nyo]

ㄴ [n] + ㅜ [u] = 누 [nu]

ㄴ [n] + ㅠ [yu] = 뉴 [nyu]

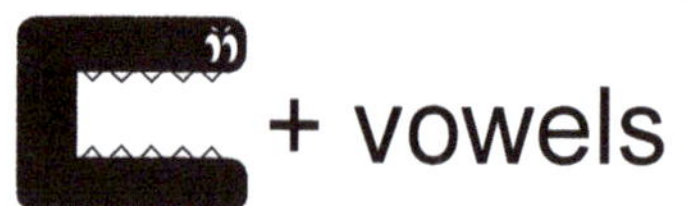

+ vowels

Write combinations of the consonant 'ㄷ' with vowels.

ㄷ [d] + ㅣ [i] = 디 [di]

ㄷ [d] + ㅏ [a] = 다 [da]

ㄷ [d] + ㅑ [ya] = 댜 [dya]

ㄷ [d] + ㅓ [eo] = 더 [deo]

ㄷ [d] + ㅕ [yeo] = 뎌 [dyeo]

ㄷ [d]
ㅡ [eu]
= [deu]

ㄷ [d]
ㅗ [o]
= [do]

ㄷ [d]
ㅛ [yo]
= [dyo]

ㄷ [d]
ㅜ [u]
= [du]

ㄷ [d]
ㅠ [yu]
= [dyu]

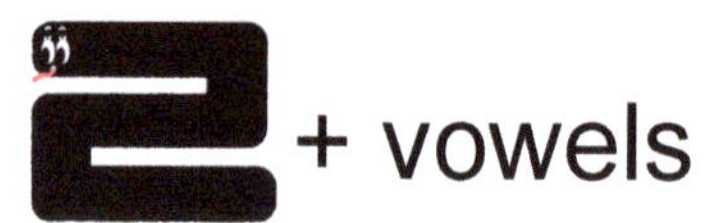

ㄹ + vowels

Write combinations of the consonant 'ㄹ' with vowels.

ㄹ [r] + ㅣ [i] = 리 [ri]

ㄹ [r] + ㅏ [a] = 라 [ra]

ㄹ [r] + ㅑ [ya] = 랴 [rya]

ㄹ [r] + ㅓ [eo] = 러 [reo]

ㄹ [r] + ㅕ [yeo] = 려 [ryeo]

ㄹ [r]
ㅡ [eu]
=
르
[reu]
ㄹ [r]
ㅗ [o]
=
로
[ro]
ㄹ [r]
ㅛ [yo]
=
료
[ryo]
ㄹ [r]
ㅜ [u]
=
루
[ru]
ㄹ [r]
ㅠ [yu]
=
류
[ryu]

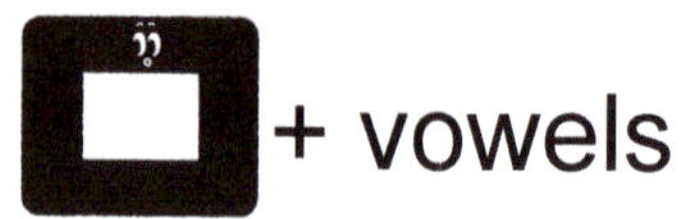

ㅁ + vowels

Write combinations of the consonant 'ㅁ' with vowels.

ㅁ [m] + ㅣ [i] = 미 [mi]

ㅁ [m] + ㅏ [a] = 마 [ma]

ㅁ [m] + ㅑ [ya] = 먀 [mya]

ㅁ [m] + ㅓ [eo] = 머 [meo]

ㅁ [m] + ㅕ [yeo] = 며 [myeo]

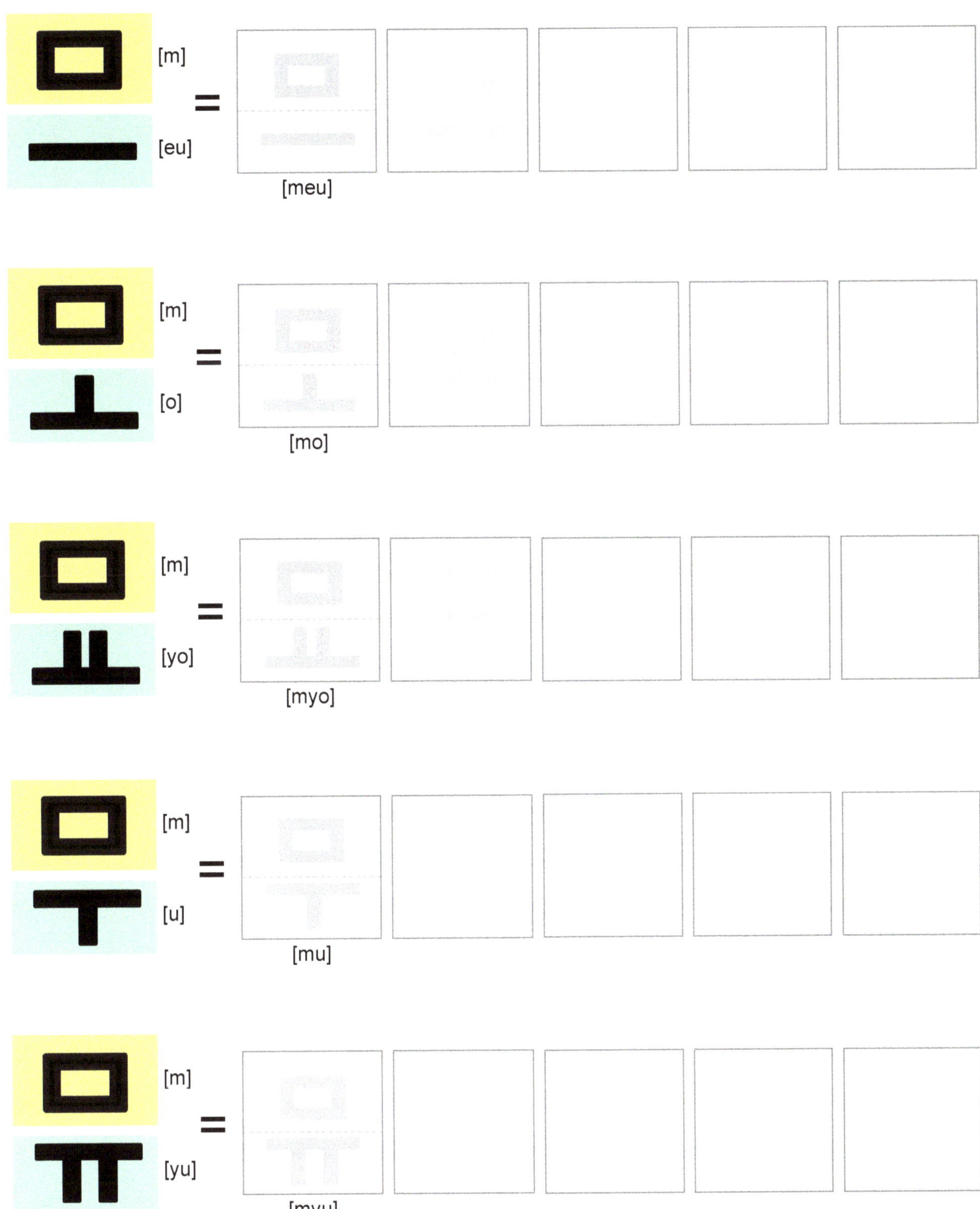
[m]
[eu]
[meu]
[m]
[o]
[mo]
[m]
[yo]
[myo]
[m]
[u]
[mu]
[m]
[yu]
[myu]

ㅂ + vowels

Write combinations of the consonant 'ㅂ' with vowels.

ㅂ [b]	ㅣ [i]	=	비 [bi]					
ㅂ [b]	ㅏ [a]	=	바 [ba]					
ㅂ [b]	ㅑ [ya]	=	뱌 [bya]					
ㅂ [b]	ㅓ [eo]	=	버 [beo]					
ㅂ [b]	ㅕ [yeo]	=	벼 [byeo]					

ㅂ [b]
ㅡ [eu]
=
[beu]
ㅂ [b]
ㅗ [o]
=
[bo]
ㅂ [b]
ㅛ [yo]
=
[byo]
ㅂ [b]
ㅜ [u]
=
[bu]
ㅂ [b]
ㅠ [yu]
=
[byu]

+ vowels

Write combinations of the consonant 'ㅅ' with vowels.

ㅅ [s] + ㅣ [i] = 시 [si]

ㅅ [s] + ㅏ [a] = 사 [sa]

ㅅ [s] + ㅑ [ya] = 샤 [sya]

ㅅ [s] + ㅓ [eo] = 서 [seo]

ㅅ [s] + ㅕ [yeo] = 셔 [syeo]

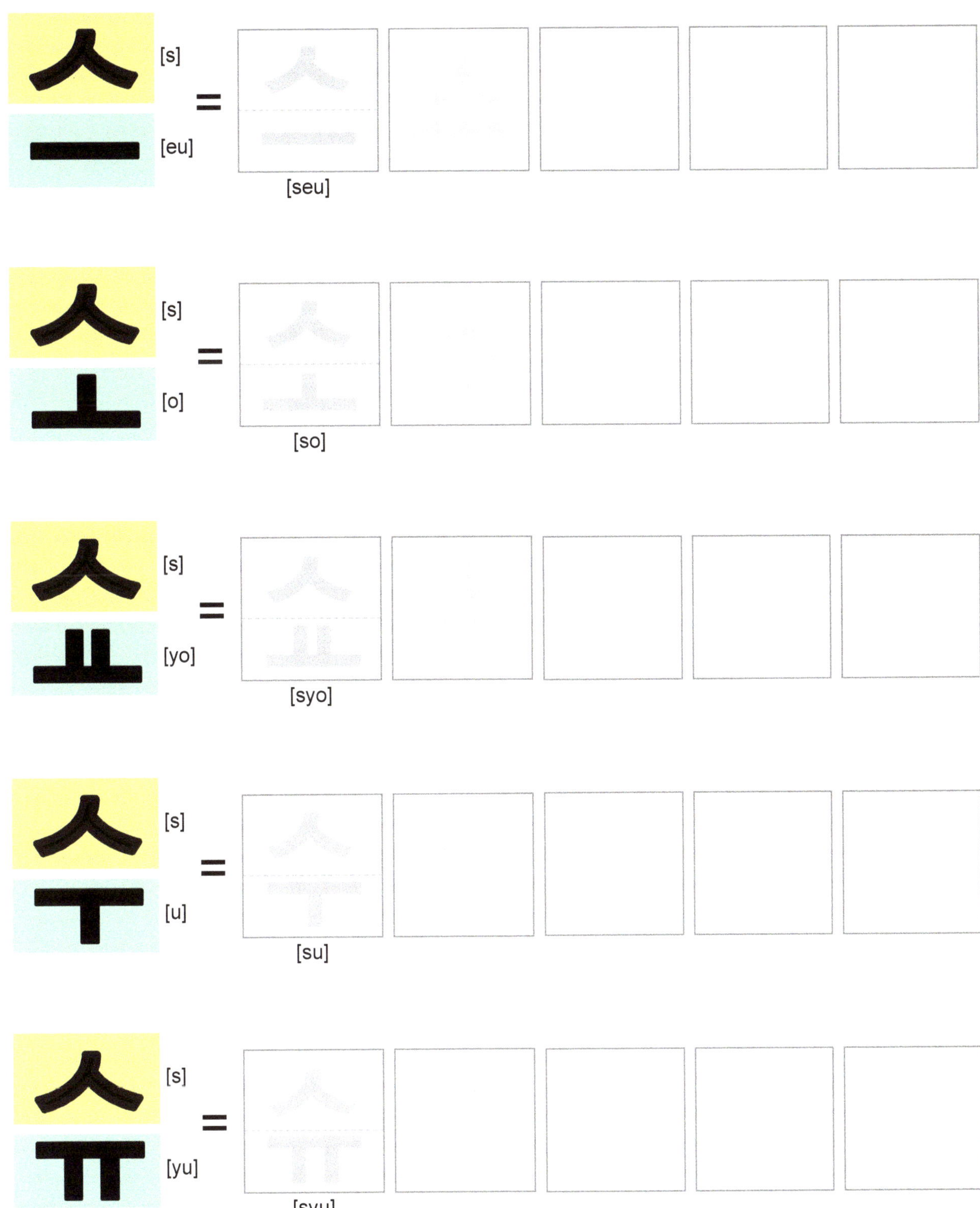
ㅅ
[s]
ㅡ
[eu]
=
[seu]
ㅅ
[s]
ㅗ
[o]
=
[so]
ㅅ
[s]
ㅛ
[yo]
=
[syo]
ㅅ
[s]
ㅜ
[u]
=
[su]
ㅅ
[s]
ㅠ
[yu]
=
[syu]

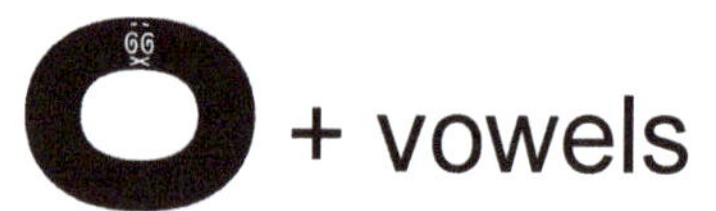

ㅇ + vowels

Write combinations of the consonant 'ㅇ' with vowels.

ㅇ ㅣ [i] = 이 [i]

ㅇ ㅏ [a] = 아 [a]

ㅇ ㅑ [ya] = 야 [ya]

ㅇ ㅓ [eo] = 어 [eo]

ㅇ ㅕ [yeo] = 여 [yeo]

ㅇ
ㅡ [eu] =
[eu]
ㅇ
ㅗ [o] =
[o]
ㅇ
ㅛ [yo] =
[yo]
ㅇ
ㅜ [u] =
[u]
ㅇ
ㅠ [yu] =
[yu]

ㅈ + vowels

Write combinations of the consonant 'ㅈ' with vowels.

ㅈ [j]	ㅣ [i]	=	지 [ji]
ㅈ [j]	ㅏ [a]	=	자 [ja]
ㅈ [j]	ㅑ [ya]	=	쟈 [jya]
ㅈ [j]	ㅓ [eo]	=	저 [jeo]
ㅈ [j]	ㅕ [yeo]	=	져 [jyeo]

ㅈ [j]
ㅡ [eu]
=
[jeu]
ㅈ [j]
ㅗ [o]
=
[jo]
ㅈ [j]
ㅛ [yo]
=
[jyo]
ㅈ [j]
ㅜ [u]
=
[ju]
ㅈ [j]
ㅠ [yu]
=
[jyu]

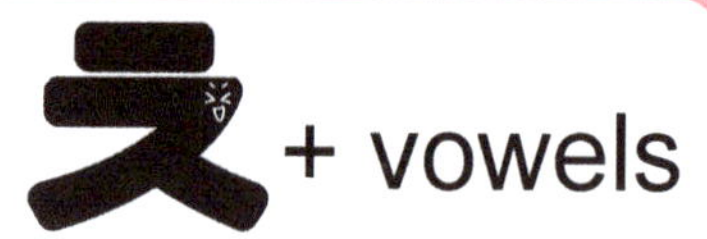

ㅊ + vowels

Write combinations of the consonant 'ㅊ' with vowels.

ㅊ [ch] + ㅣ [i] = 치 [chi]

ㅊ [ch] + ㅏ [a] = 차 [cha]

ㅊ [ch] + ㅑ [ya] = 챠 [chya]

ㅊ [ch] + ㅓ [eo] = 처 [cheo]

ㅊ [ch] + ㅕ [yeo] = 쳐 [chyeo]

ㅊ
[ch]
=
ㅡ
[eu]
츠
[cheu]
ㅊ
[ch]
=
ㅗ
[o]
초
[cho]
ㅊ
[ch]
=
ㅛ
[yo]
쵸
[chyo]
ㅊ
[ch]
=
ㅜ
[u]
추
[chu]
ㅊ
[ch]
=
ㅠ
[yu]
츄
[chyu]

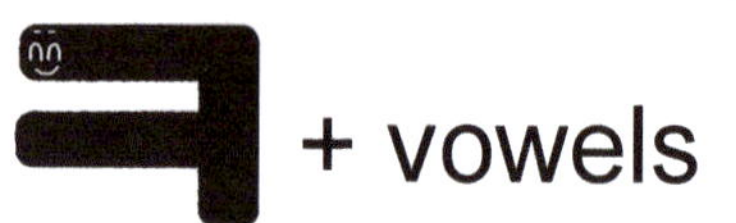

ㅋ + vowels

Write combinations of the consonant 'ㅋ' with vowels.

ㅋ [k] + ㅣ [i] = 키 [ki]

ㅋ [k] + ㅏ [a] = 카 [ka]

ㅋ [k] + ㅑ [ya] = 캬 [kya]

ㅋ [k] + ㅓ [eo] = 커 [keo]

ㅋ [k] + ㅕ [yeo] = 켜 [kyeo]

ㅋ [k]
ㅡ [eu]
=
[keu]
ㅋ [k]
ㅗ [o]
=
[ko]
ㅋ [k]
ㅛ [yo]
=
[kyo]
ㅋ [k]
ㅜ [u]
=
[ku]
ㅋ [k]
ㅠ [yu]
=
[kyu]

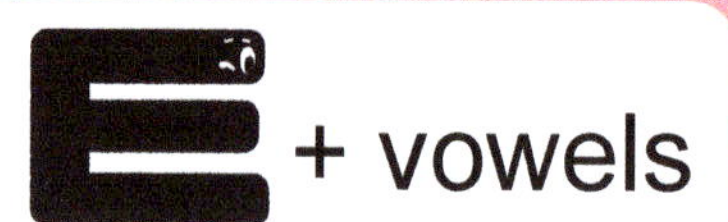

ㅌ + vowels

Write combinations of the consonant 'ㅌ' with vowels.

ㅌ [t] + ㅣ [i] = 티 [ti]

ㅌ [t] + ㅏ [a] = 타 [ta]

ㅌ [t] + ㅑ [ya] = 탸 [tya]

ㅌ [t] + ㅓ [eo] = 터 [teo]

ㅌ [t] + ㅕ [yeo] = 텨 [tyeo]

ㅌ [t] + ㅡ [eu] = 트 [teu]

ㅌ [t] + ㅗ [o] = 토 [to]

ㅌ [t] + ㅛ [yo] = 툐 [tyo]

ㅌ [t] + ㅜ [u] = 투 [tu]

ㅌ [t] + ㅠ [yu] = 튜 [tyu]

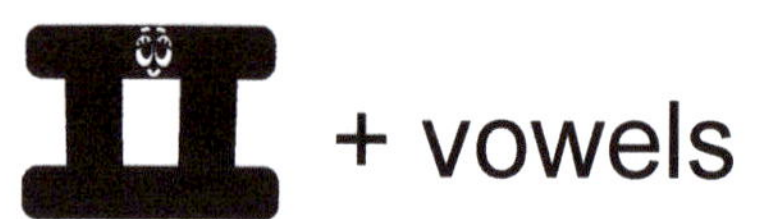

ㅍ + vowels

Write combinations of the consonant 'ㅍ' with vowels.

ㅍ [p] + ㅣ [i] = 피 [pi]

ㅍ [p] + ㅏ [a] = 파 [pa]

ㅍ [p] + ㅑ [ya] = 퍄 [pya]

ㅍ [p] + ㅓ [eo] = 퍼 [peo]

ㅍ [p] + ㅕ [yeo] = 펴 [pyeo]

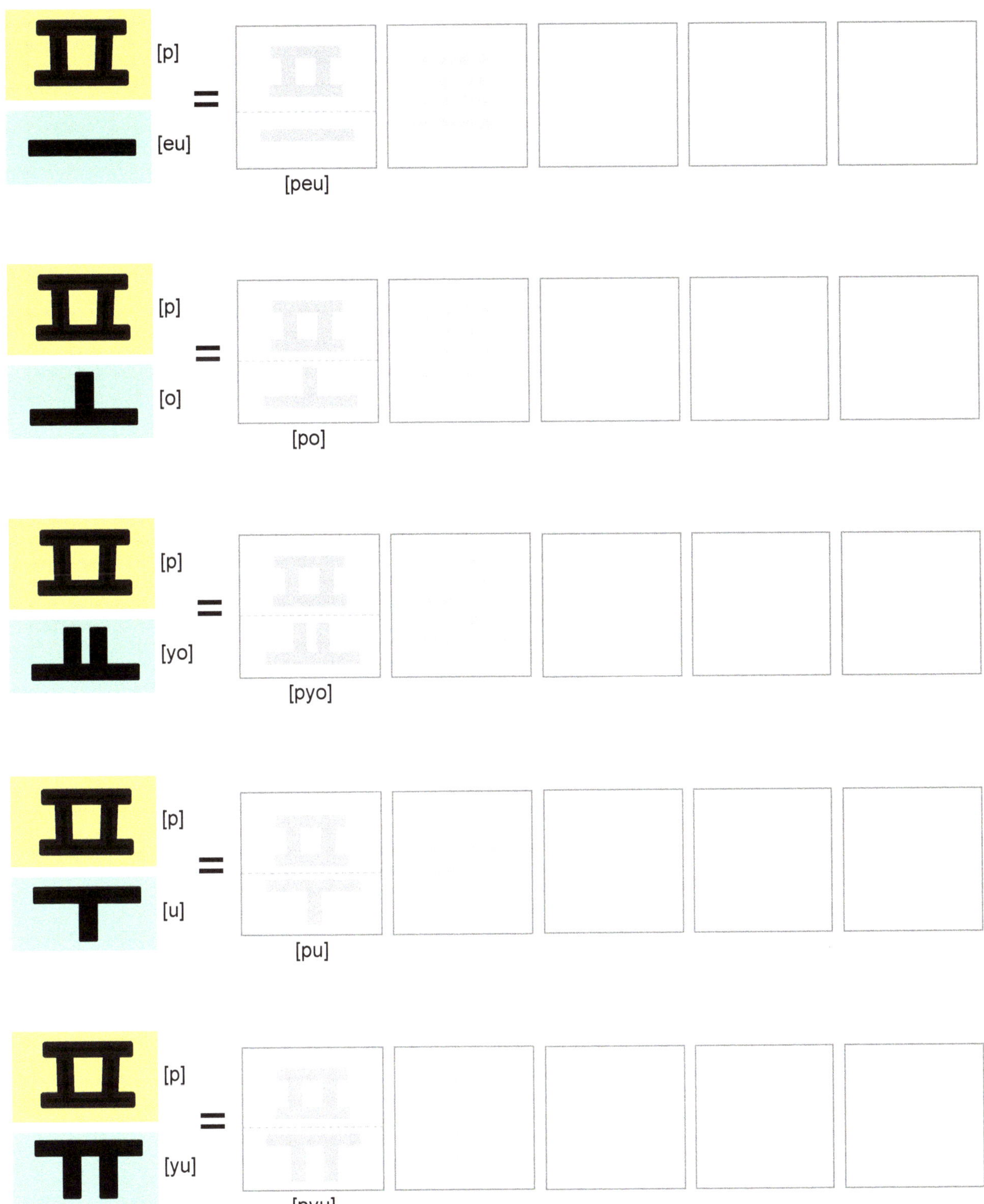
ㅍ [p]
ㅡ [eu]
=
[peu]
ㅍ [p]
ㅗ [o]
=
[po]
ㅍ [p]
ㅛ [yo]
=
[pyo]
ㅍ [p]
ㅜ [u]
=
[pu]
ㅍ [p]
ㅠ [yu]
=
[pyu]

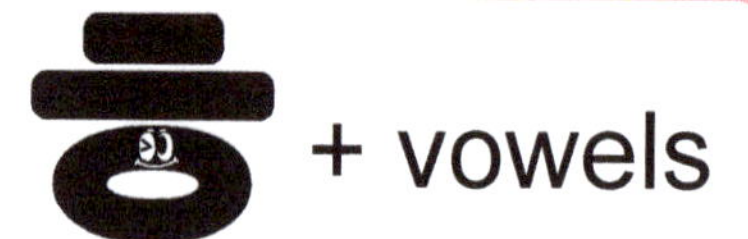

+ vowels

Write combinations of the consonant 'ㅎ' with vowels.

ㅎ	ㅣ	=	히				
[h]	[i]		[hi]				

ㅎ	ㅏ	=	하				
[h]	[a]		[ha]				

ㅎ	ㅑ	=	햐				
[h]	[ya]		[hya]				

ㅎ	ㅓ	=	허				
[h]	[eo]		[heo]				

ㅎ	ㅕ	=	혀				
[h]	[yeo]		[hyeo]				

ㅎ [h]
ㅡ [eu]
=
흐
[heu]
ㅎ [h]
ㅗ [o]
=
호
[ho]
ㅎ [h]
ㅛ [yo]
=
효
[hyo]
ㅎ [h]
ㅜ [u]
=
후
[hu]
ㅎ [h]
ㅠ [yu]
=
휴
[hyu]

Review

Write combinations of consonants and vowels.

V / C	ㅣ 이 [i]	ㅏ 아 [a]	ㅑ 야 [ya]	ㅓ 어 [eo]	ㅕ 여 [yeo]	ㅡ 으 [eu]	ㅗ 오 [o]	ㅛ 요 [yo]	ㅜ 우 [u]	ㅠ 유 [yu]
ㄱ 기역 [g]										
ㄴ 니은 [n]										
ㄷ 디귿 [d]										
ㄹ 리을 [r]										
ㅁ 미음 [m]										
ㅂ 비읍 [b]										
ㅅ 시옷 [s]										
ㅇ 이응 [-]										
ㅈ 지읒 [j]										
ㅊ 치읓 [ch]										
ㅋ 키읔 [k]										
ㅌ 티읕 [t]										
ㅍ 피읖 [p]										
ㅎ 히읗 [h]										

Let's practice writing one more time!

C \ V	ㅣ 이 [i]	ㅏ 아 [a]	ㅑ 야 [ya]	ㅓ 어 [eo]	ㅕ 여 [yeo]	ㅡ 으 [eu]	ㅗ 오 [o]	ㅛ 요 [yo]	ㅜ 우 [u]	ㅠ 유 [yu]
ㄱ 기역 [g]										
ㄴ 니은 [n]										
ㄷ 디귿 [d]										
ㄹ 리을 [r]										
ㅁ 미음 [m]										
ㅂ 비읍 [b]										
ㅅ 시옷 [s]										
ㅇ 이응 [-]										
ㅈ 지읒 [j]										
ㅊ 치읓 [ch]										
ㅋ 키읔 [k]										
ㅌ 티읕 [t]										
ㅍ 피읖 [p]										
ㅎ 히읗 [h]										

Review

Write combinations of consonants and vowels.

C \ V	ㅏ 아 [a]	ㅑ 야 [ya]	ㅓ 어 [eo]	ㅕ 여 [yeo]	ㅗ 오 [o]	ㅛ 요 [yo]	ㅜ 우 [u]	ㅠ 유 [yu]	ㅡ 으 [eu]	ㅣ 이 [i]
ㄱ 기역 [g]										
ㄴ 니은 [n]										
ㄷ 디귿 [d]										
ㄹ 리을 [r]										
ㅁ 미음 [m]										
ㅂ 비읍 [b]										
ㅅ 시옷 [s]										
ㅇ 이응 [-]										
ㅈ 지읒 [j]										
ㅊ 치읓 [ch]										
ㅋ 키읔 [k]										
ㅌ 티읕 [t]										
ㅍ 피읖 [p]										
ㅎ 히읗 [h]										

Let's practice writing one more time!

C \ V	ㅏ 아 [a]	ㅑ 야 [ya]	ㅓ 어 [eo]	ㅕ 여 [yeo]	ㅗ 오 [o]	ㅛ 요 [yo]	ㅜ 우 [u]	ㅠ 유 [yu]	ㅡ 으 [eu]	ㅣ 이 [i]
ㄱ 기역 [g]										
ㄴ 니은 [n]										
ㄷ 디귿 [d]										
ㄹ 리을 [rl]										
ㅁ 미음 [m]										
ㅂ 비읍 [b]										
ㅅ 시옷 [s]										
ㅇ 이응 [-]										
ㅈ 지읒 [j]										
ㅊ 치읓 [ch]										
ㅋ 키읔 [k]										
ㅌ 티읕 [t]										
ㅍ 피읖 [p]										
ㅎ 히읗 [h]										

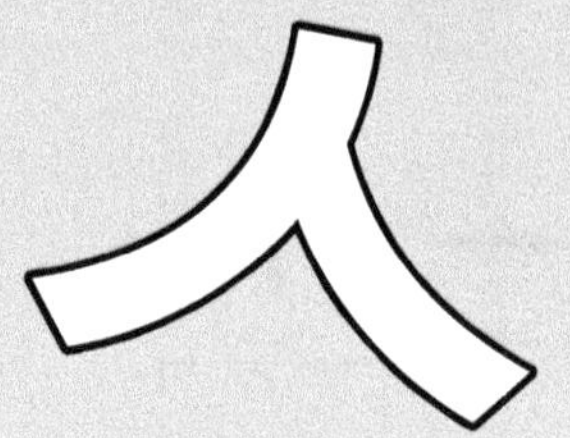

Chapter4

단어카드

Korean Word Cards

Korean Word Card

Color the ㄱ words and pictures, then cut and fold them to make Korean word cards.

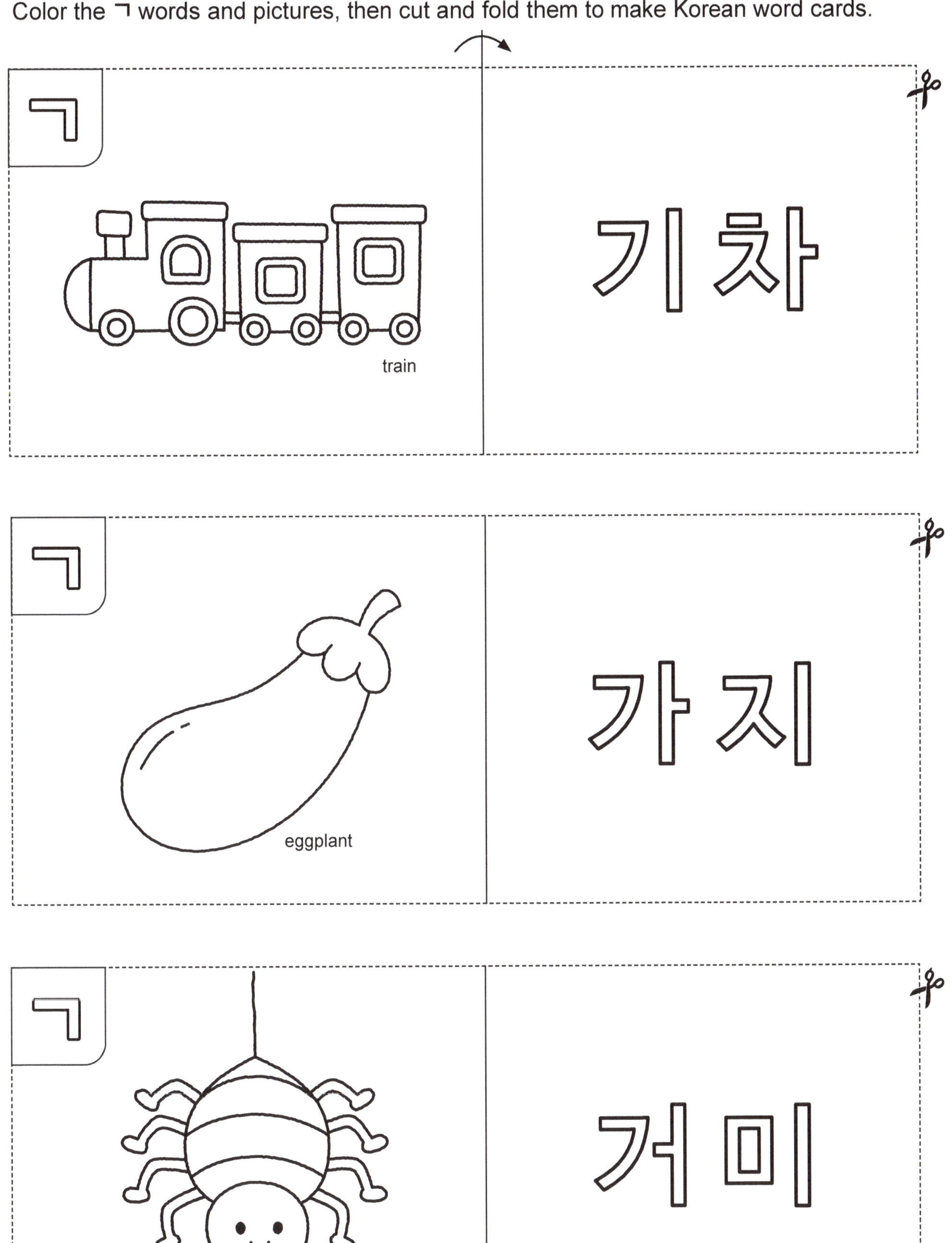

Korean Word Card

Color the ㄴ words and pictures, then cut and fold them to make Korean word cards.

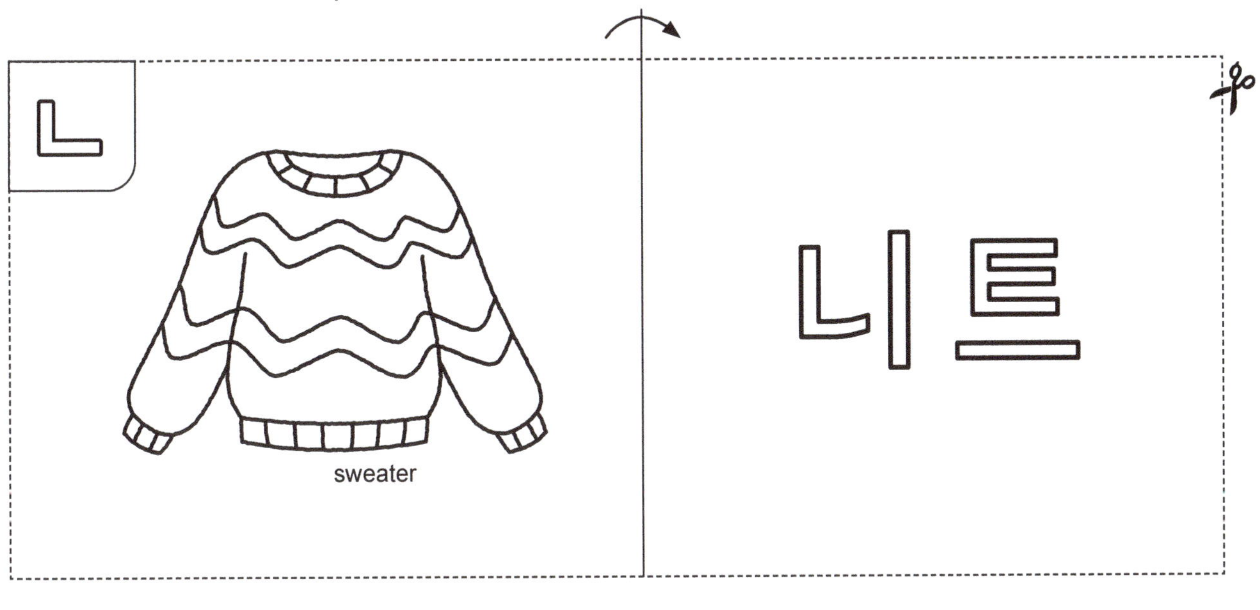

Korean Word Card

Color the ㄷ words and pictures, then cut and fold them to make Korean word cards.

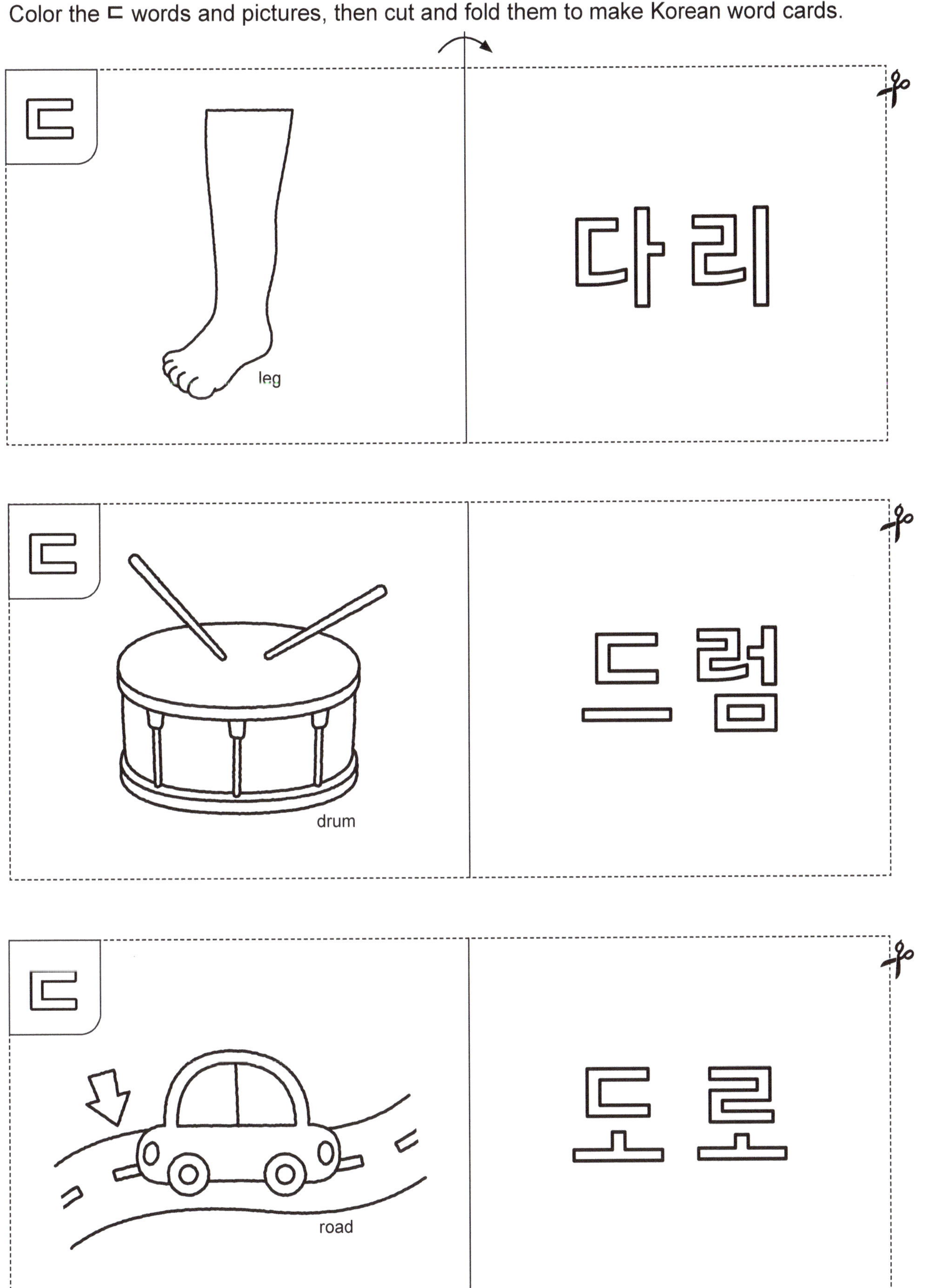

Korean Word Card

Color the ㄹ words and pictures, then cut and fold them to make Korean word cards.

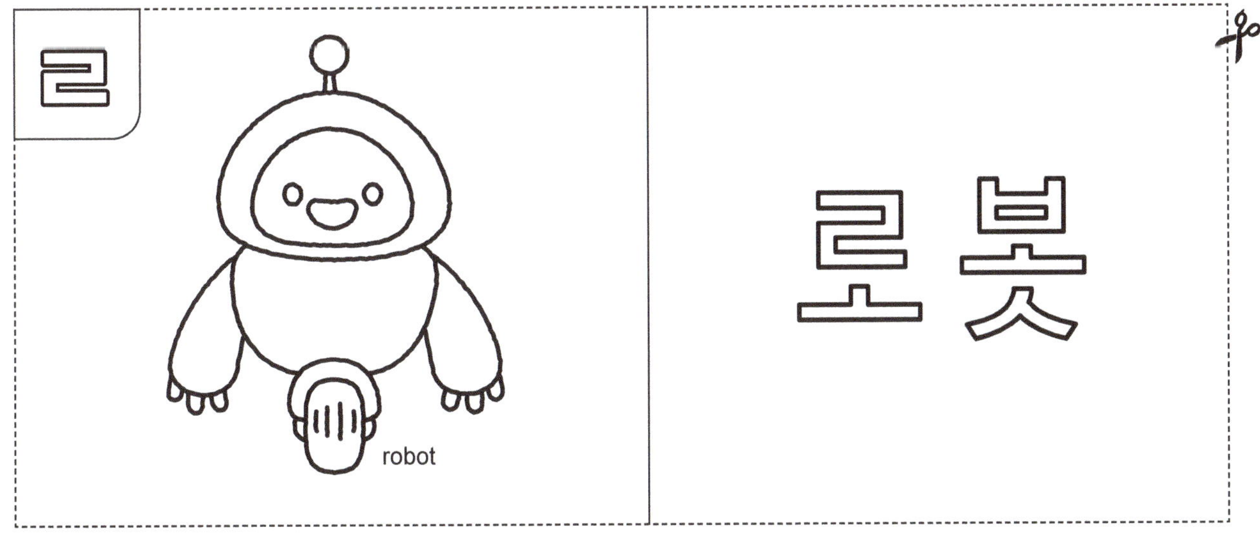

Korean Word Card

Color the ㅁ words and pictures, then cut and fold them to make Korean word cards.

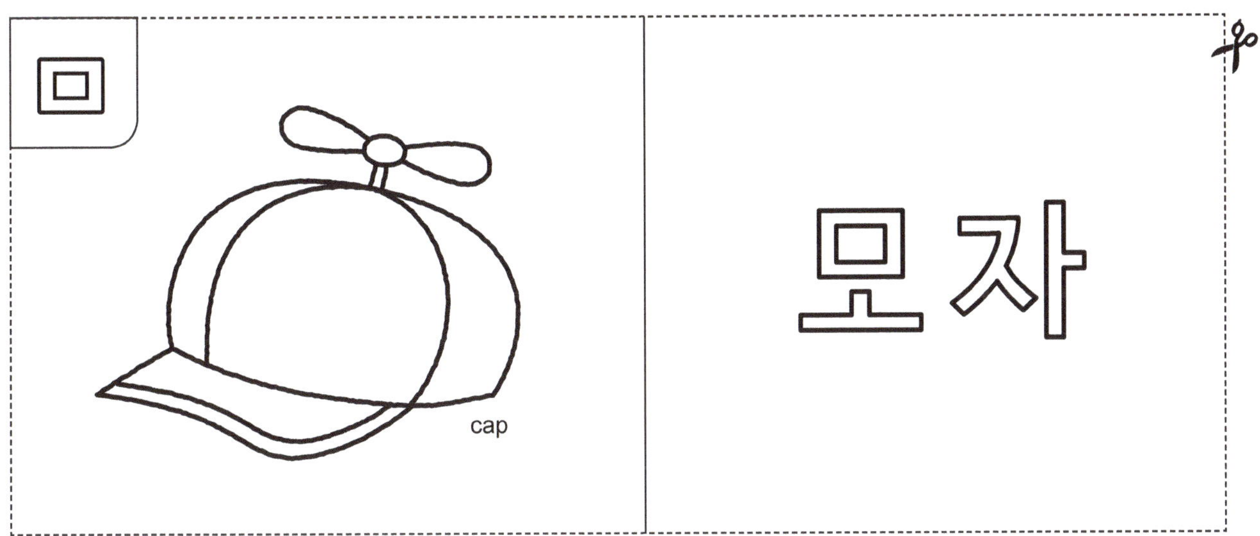

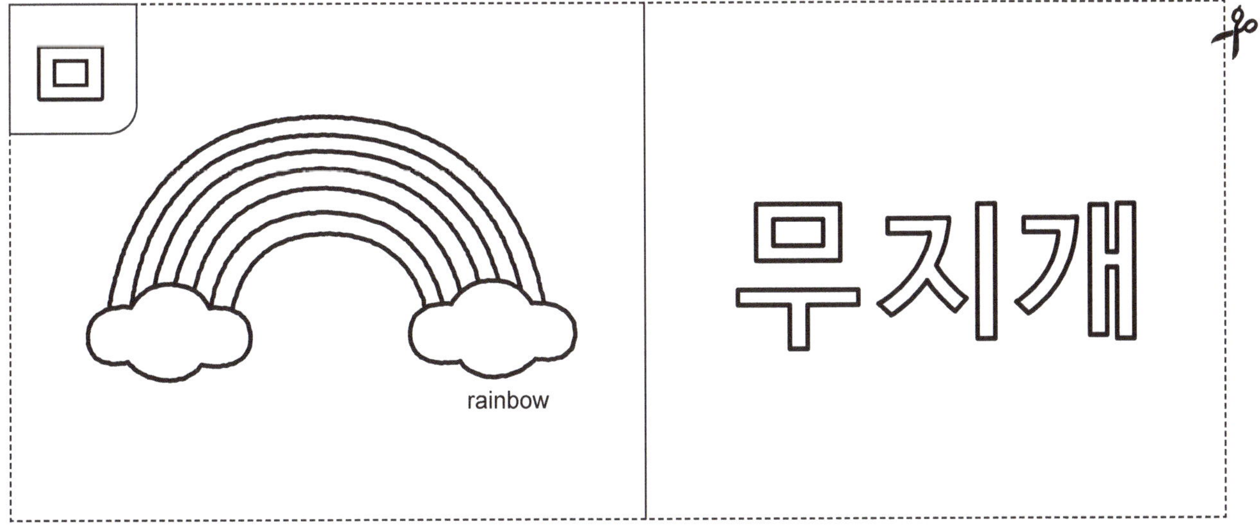

Korean Word Card

Color the ㅂ words and pictures, then cut and fold them to make Korean word cards.

Korean Word Card

Color the ㅅ words and pictures, then cut and fold them to make Korean word cards.

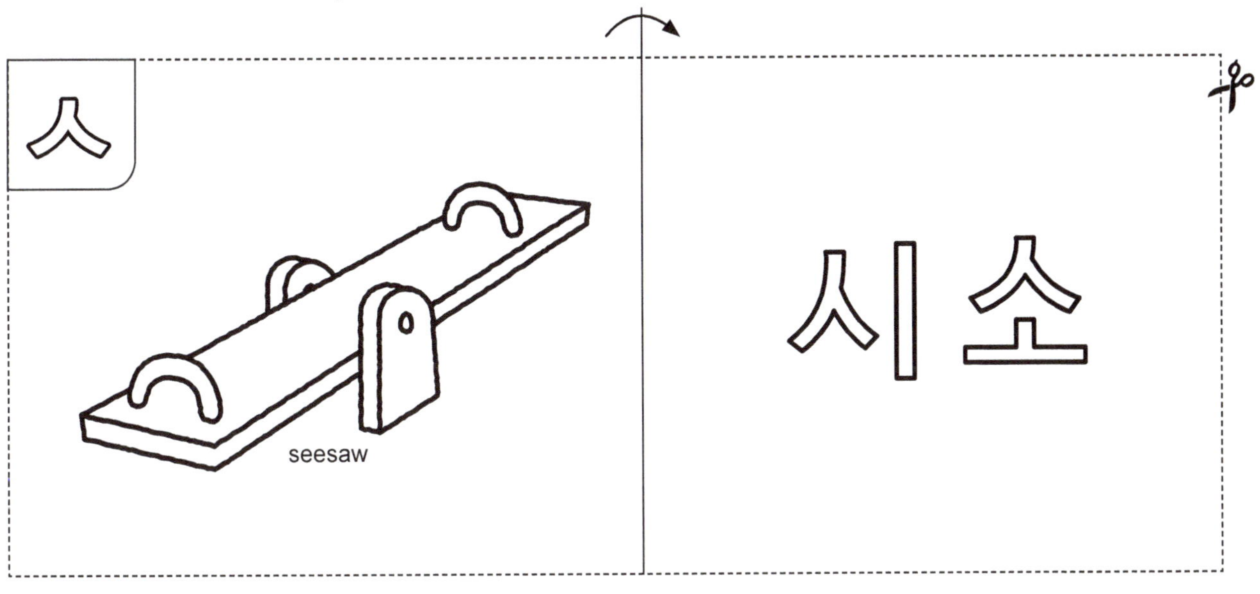

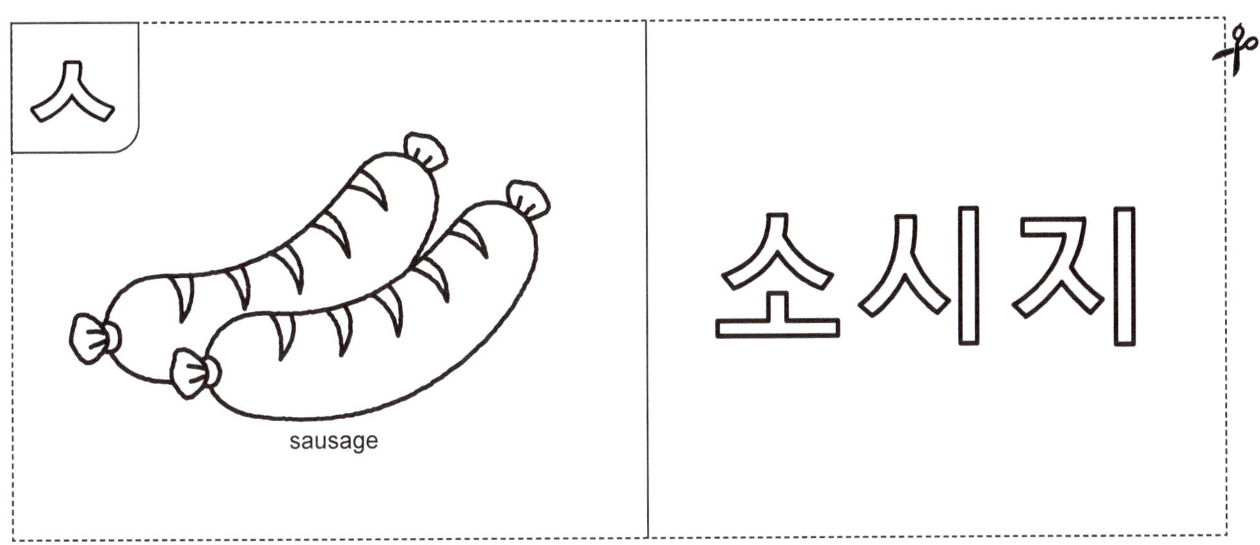

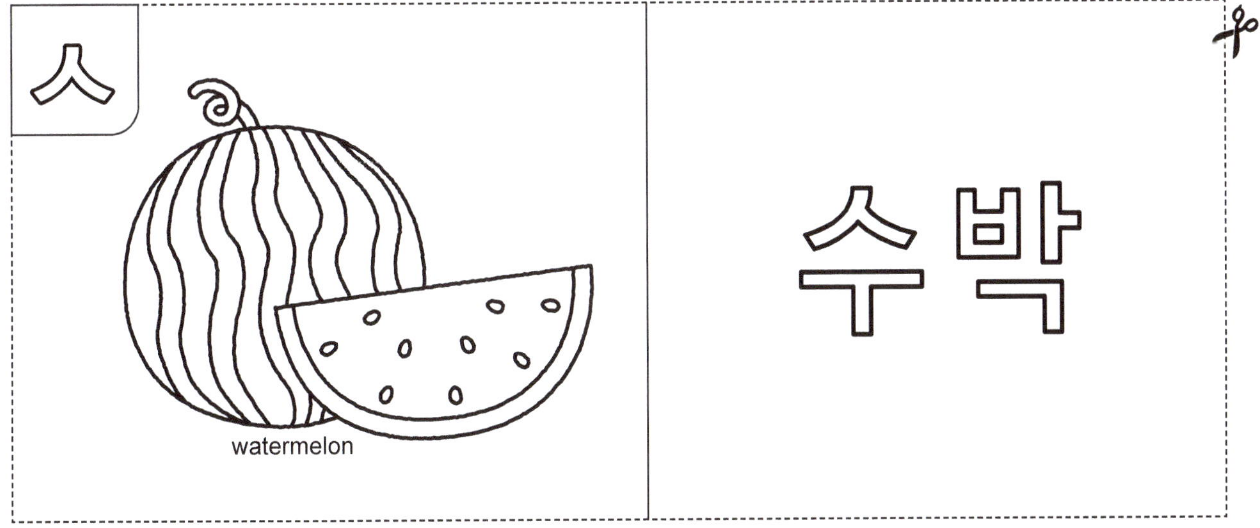

Korean Word Card

Color the ㅇ words and pictures, then cut and fold them to make Korean word cards.

Korean Word Card

Color the ㅈ words and pictures, then cut and fold them to make Korean word cards.

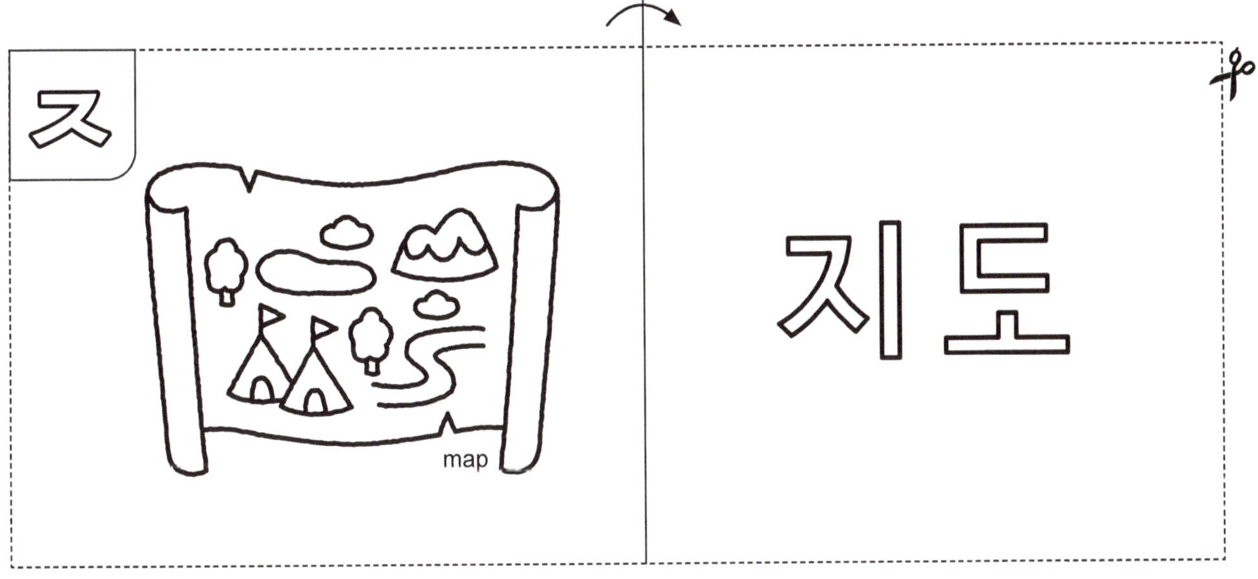

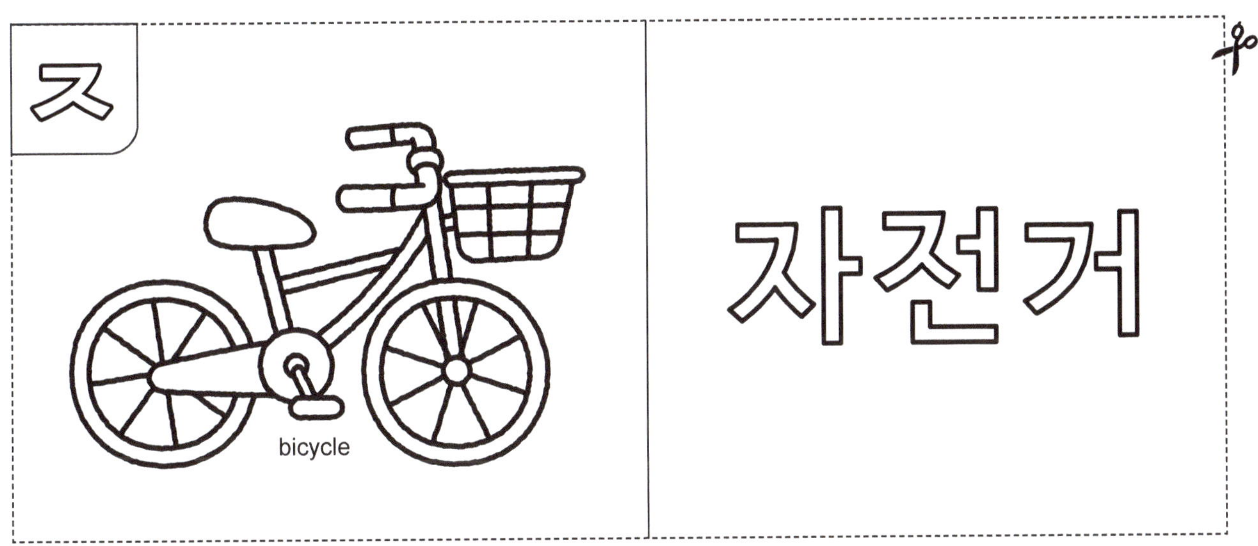

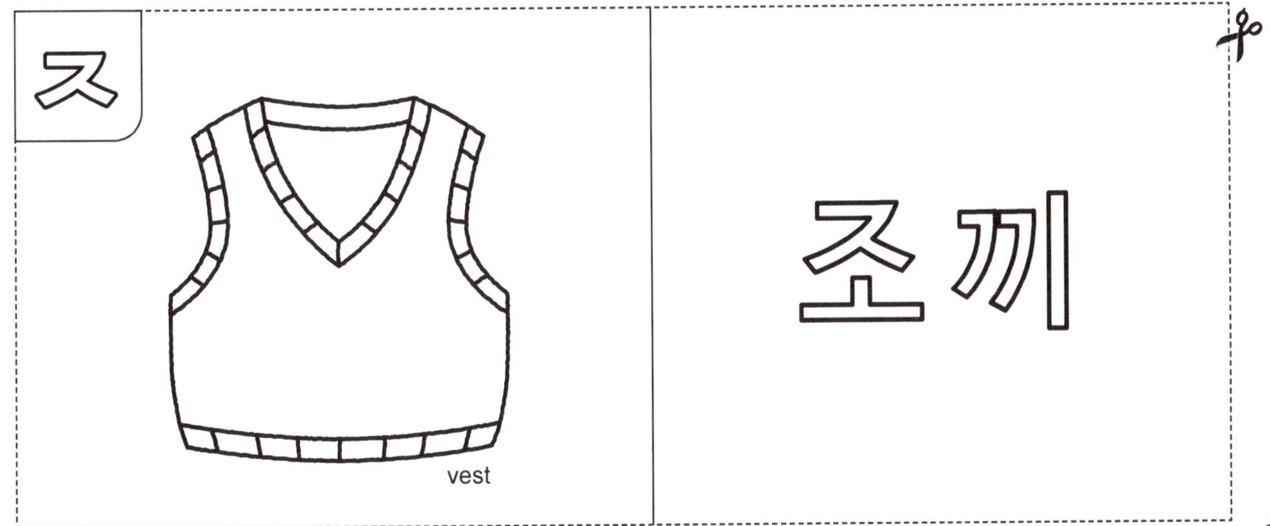

Korean Word Card

Color the ㅊ words and pictures, then cut and fold them to make Korean word cards.

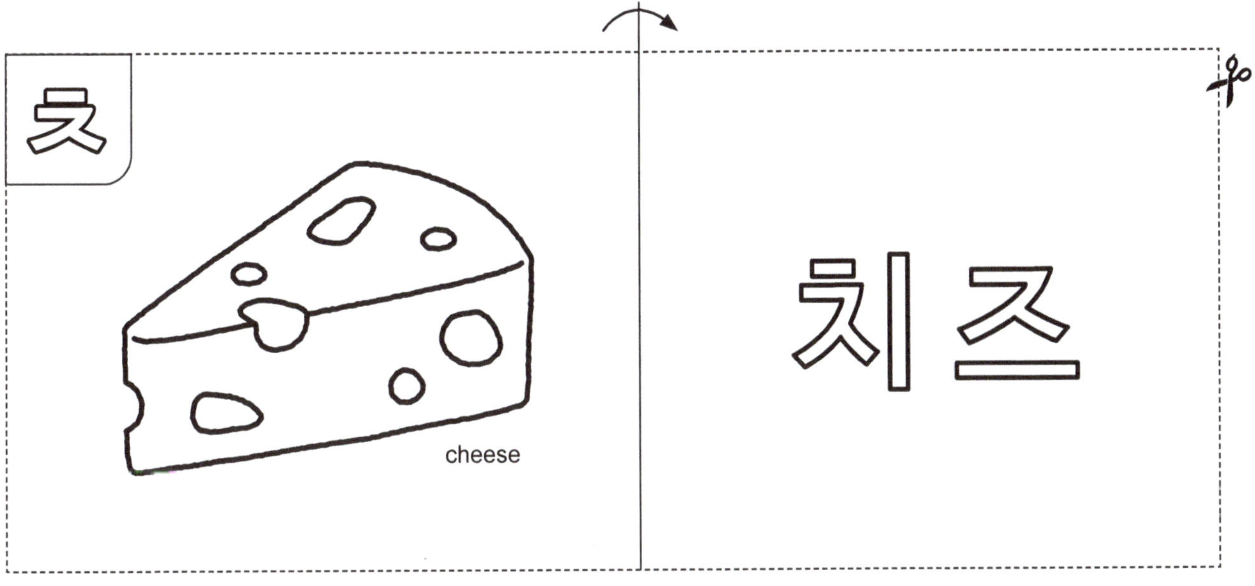

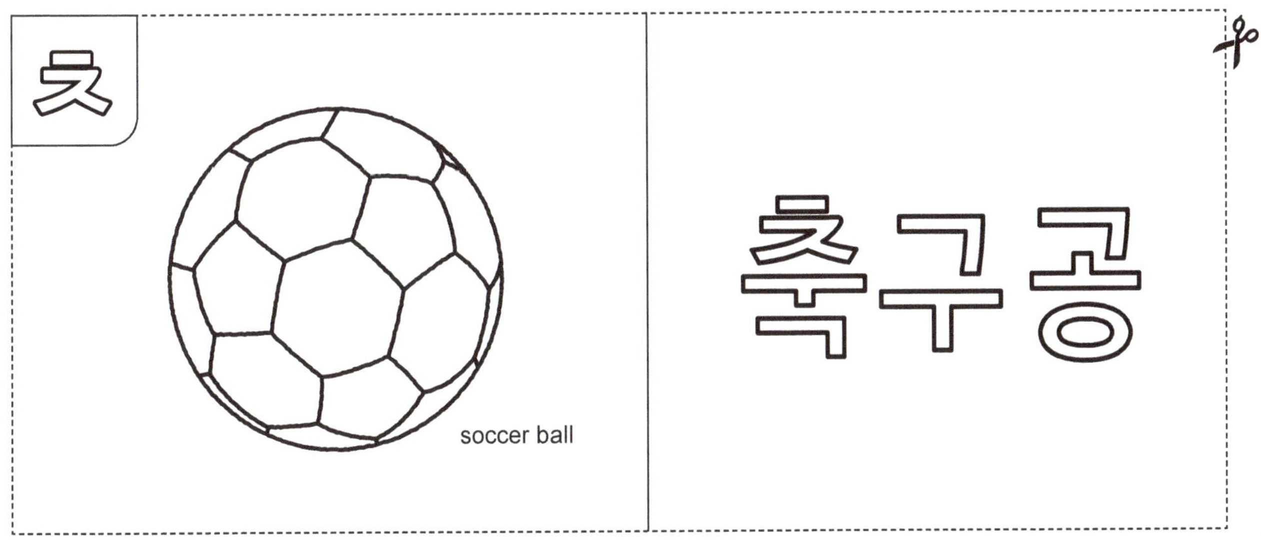

Korean Word Card

Color the ㅋ words and pictures, then cut and fold them to make Korean word cards.

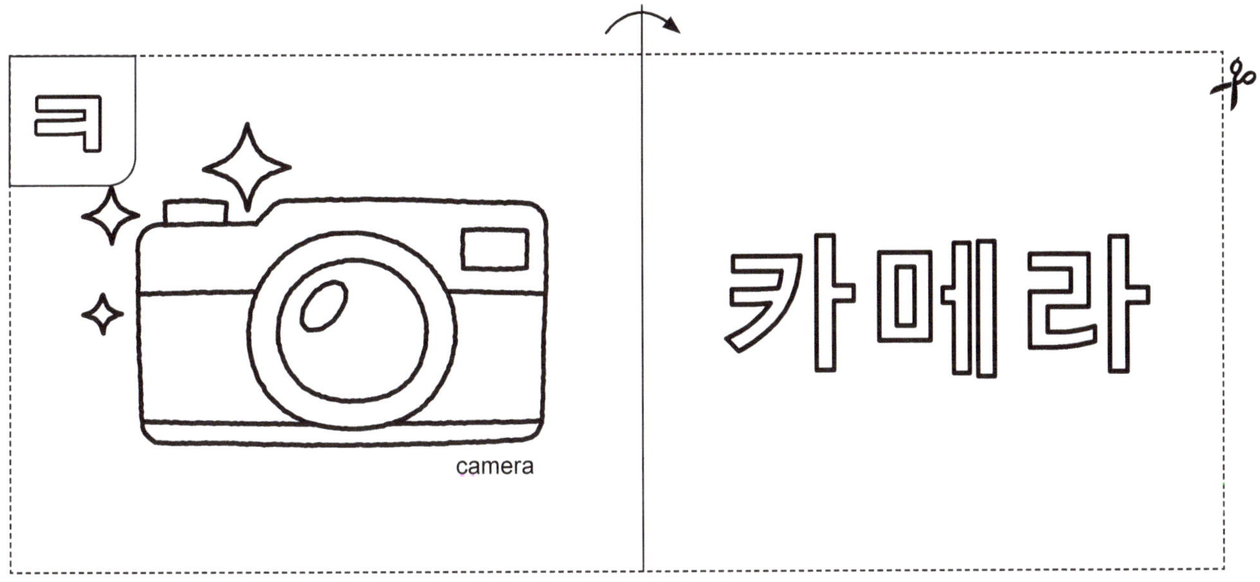

Korean Word Card

Color the ㅌ words and pictures, then cut and fold them to make Korean word cards.

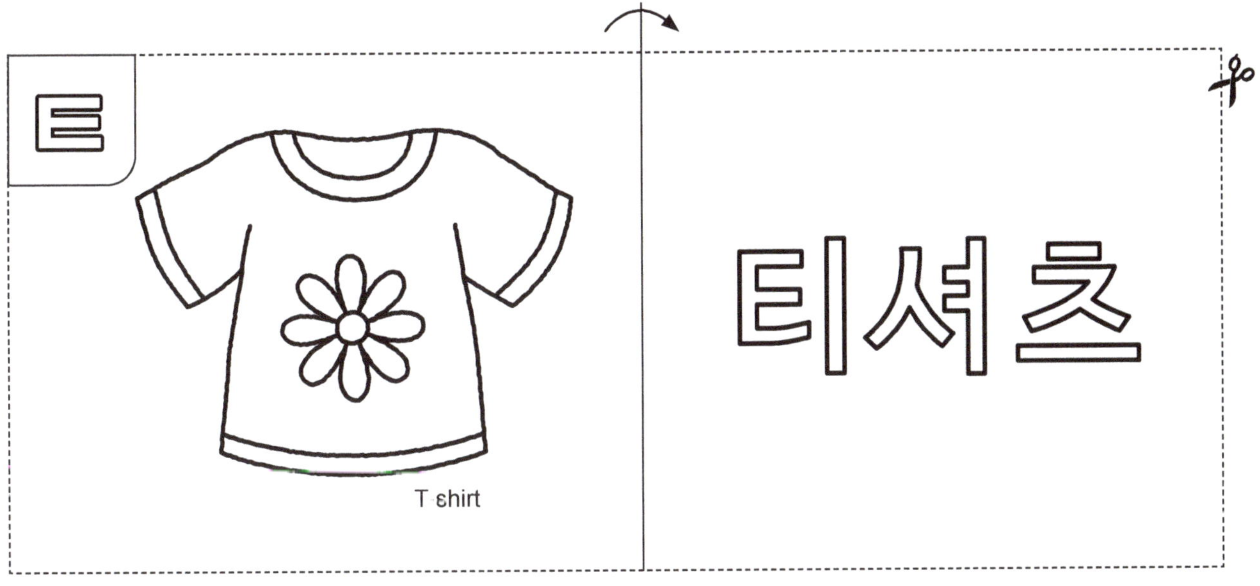

Korean Word Card

Color the ㅍ words and pictures, then cut and fold them to make Korean word cards.

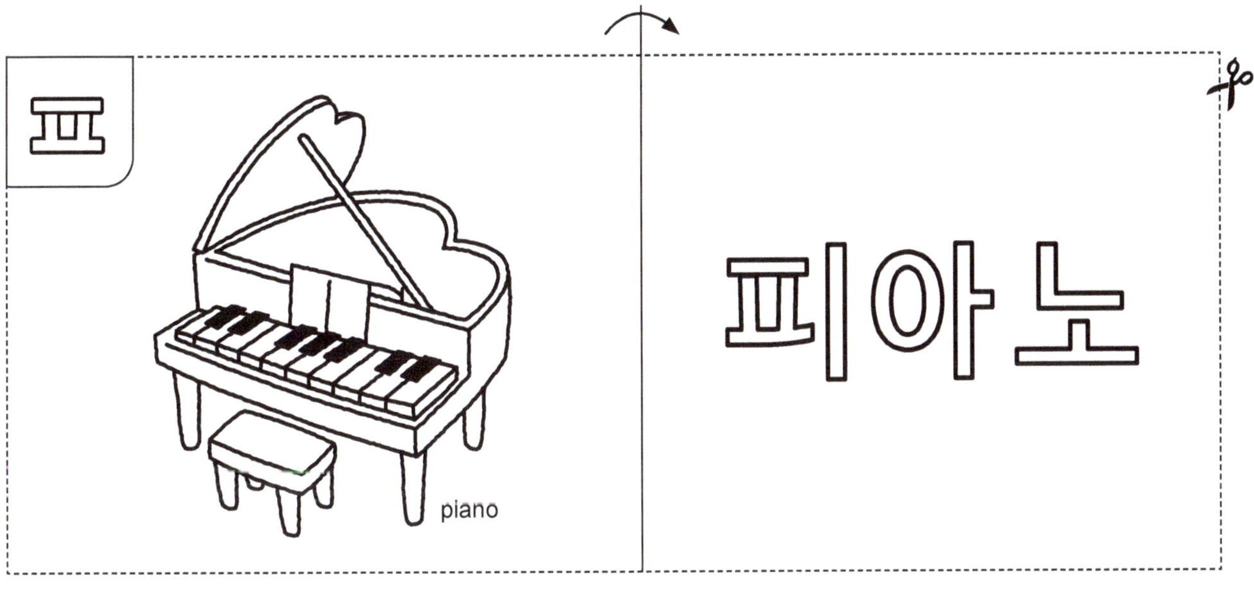

Korean Word Card

Color the ㅎ words and pictures, then cut and fold them to make Korean word cards.

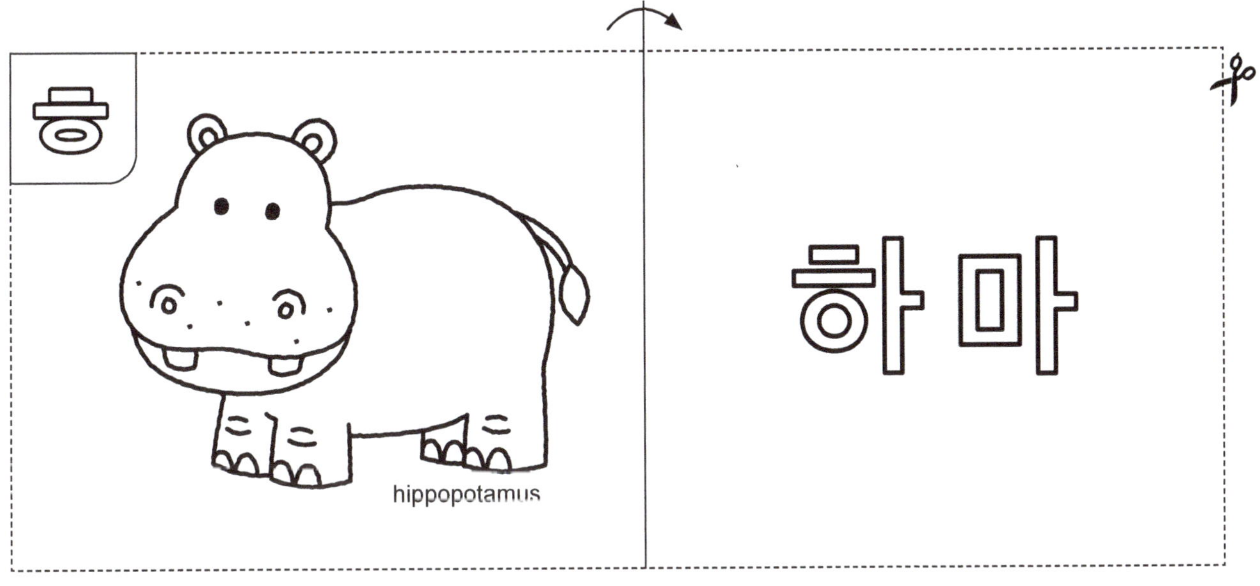

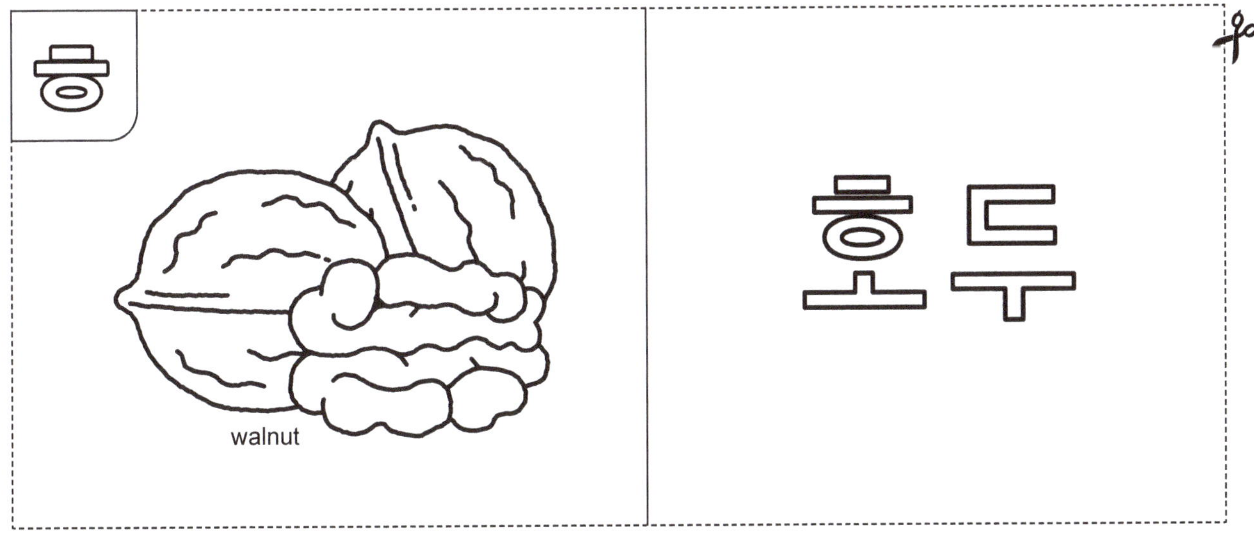

Korean Word Card

Color the ㅣ words and pictures, then cut and fold them to make Korean word cards.

Korean Word Card

Color the ㅏ words and pictures, then cut and fold them to make Korean word cards.

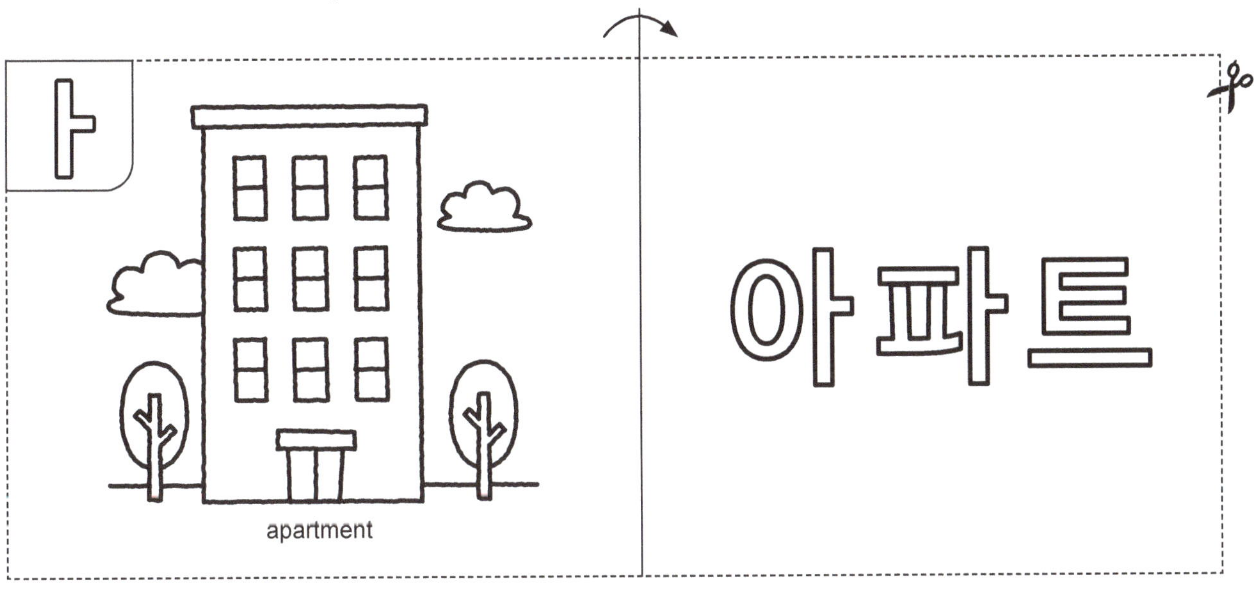

Korean Word Card

Color the ㅑ words and pictures, then cut and fold them to make Korean word cards.

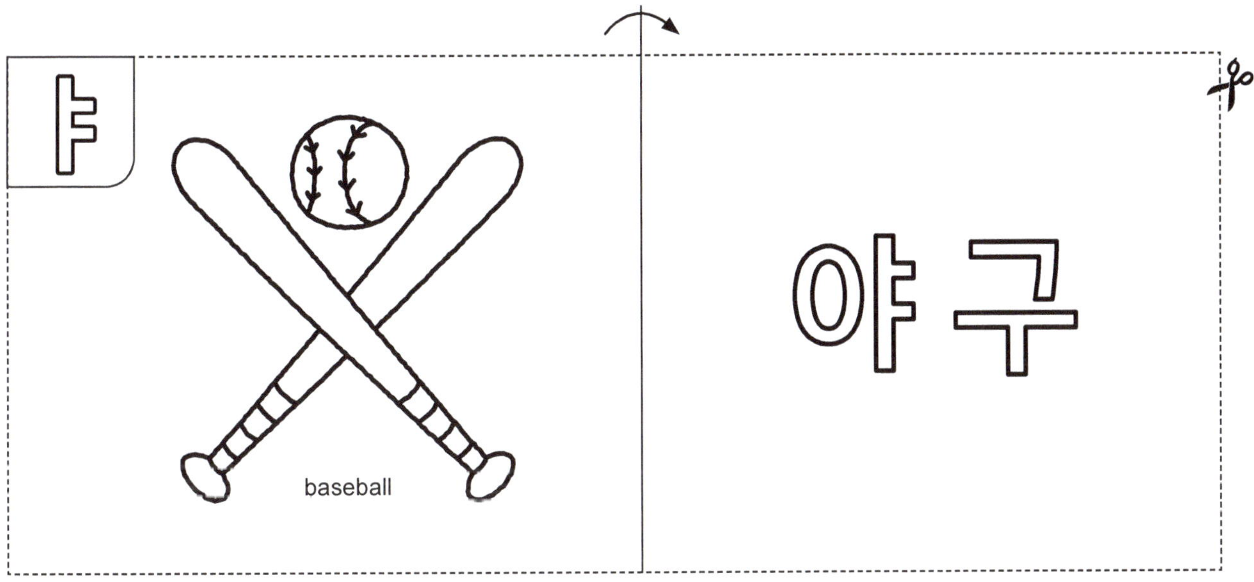

Korean Word Card

Color the ㅓ words and pictures, then cut and fold them to make Korean word cards.

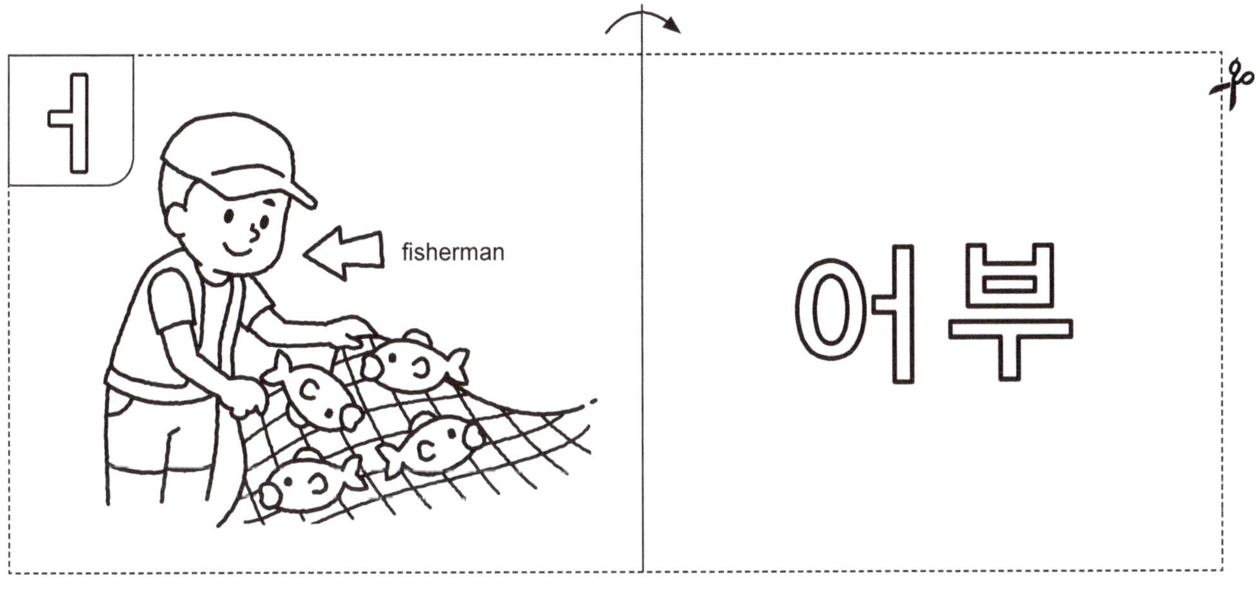

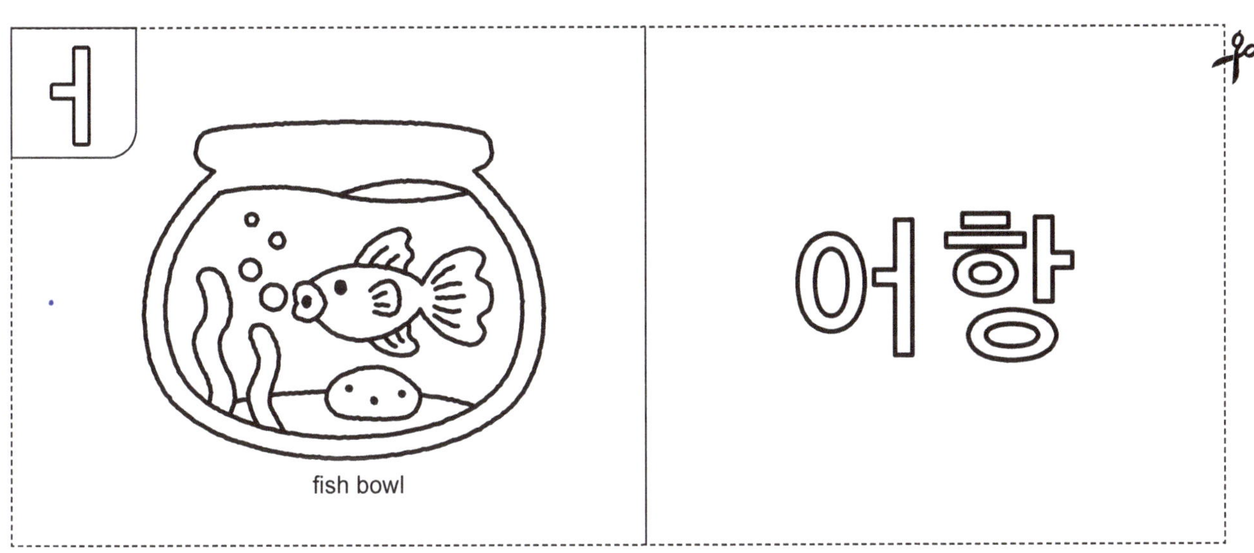

fish bowl

Korean Word Card

Color the ㅕ words and pictures, then cut and fold them to make Korean word cards.

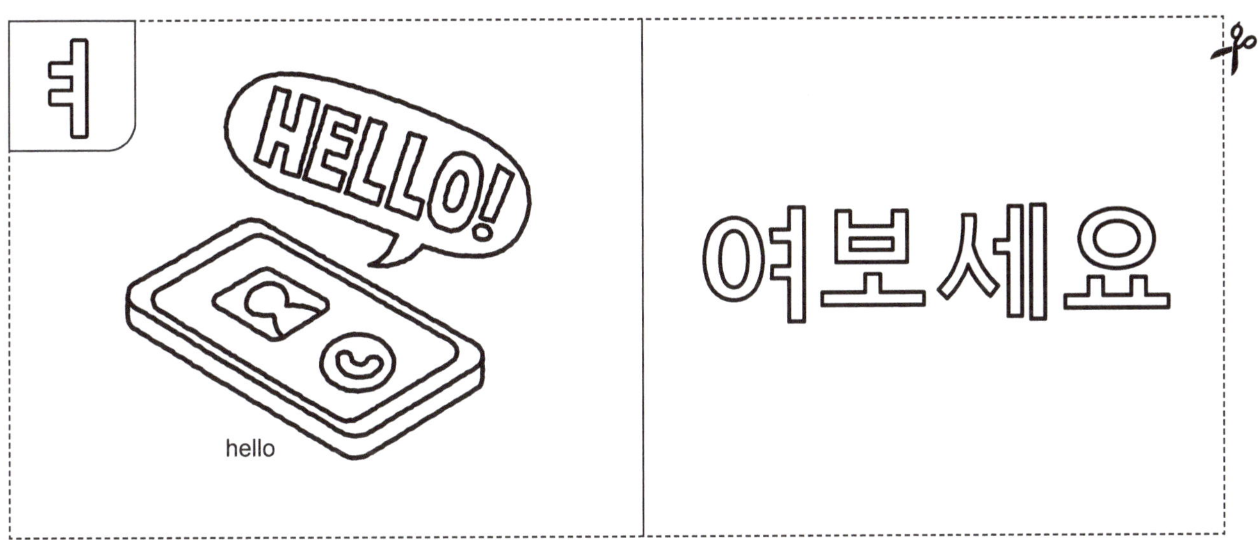

Korean Word Card

Color the ㅡ words and pictures, then cut and fold them to make Korean word cards.

Korean Word Card

Color the ㅗ words and pictures, then cut and fold them to make Korean word cards.

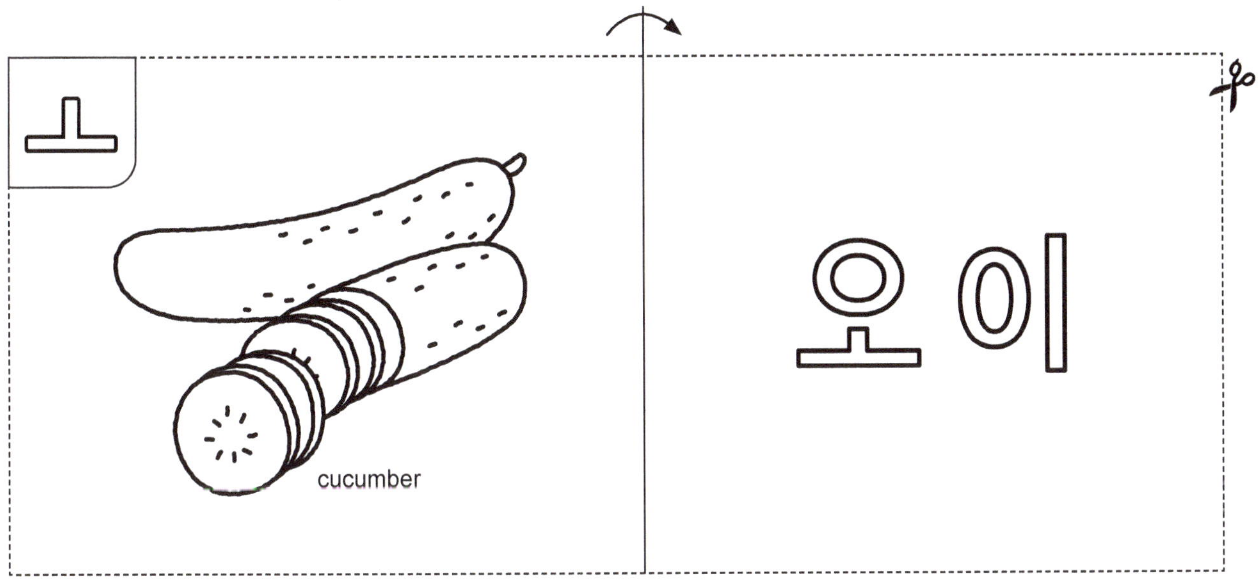

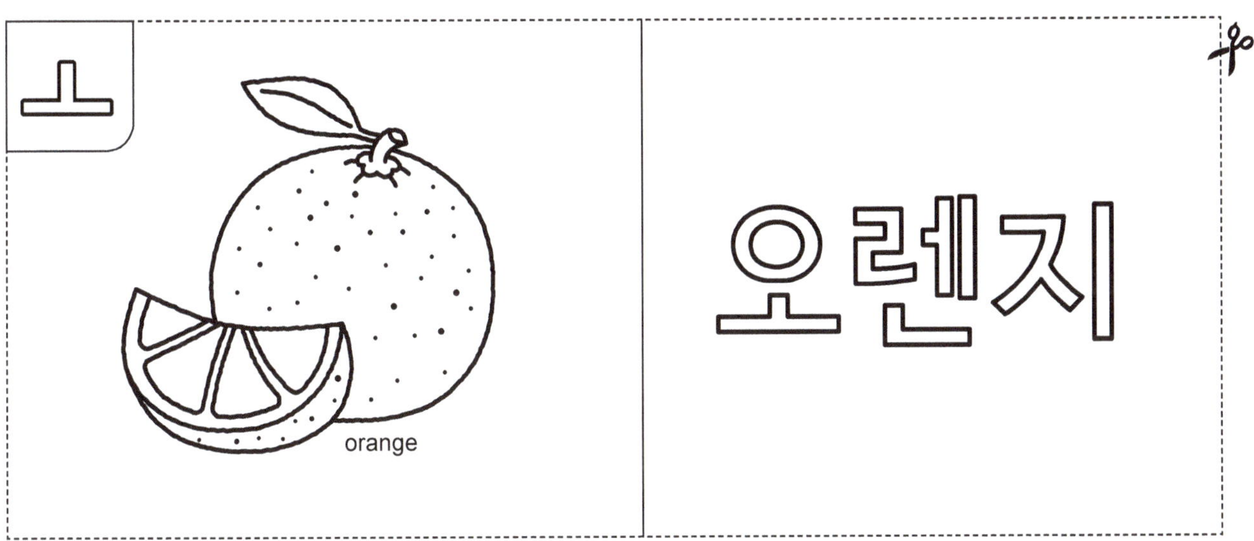

Korean Word Card

Color the ㅛ words and pictures, then cut and fold them to make Korean word cards.

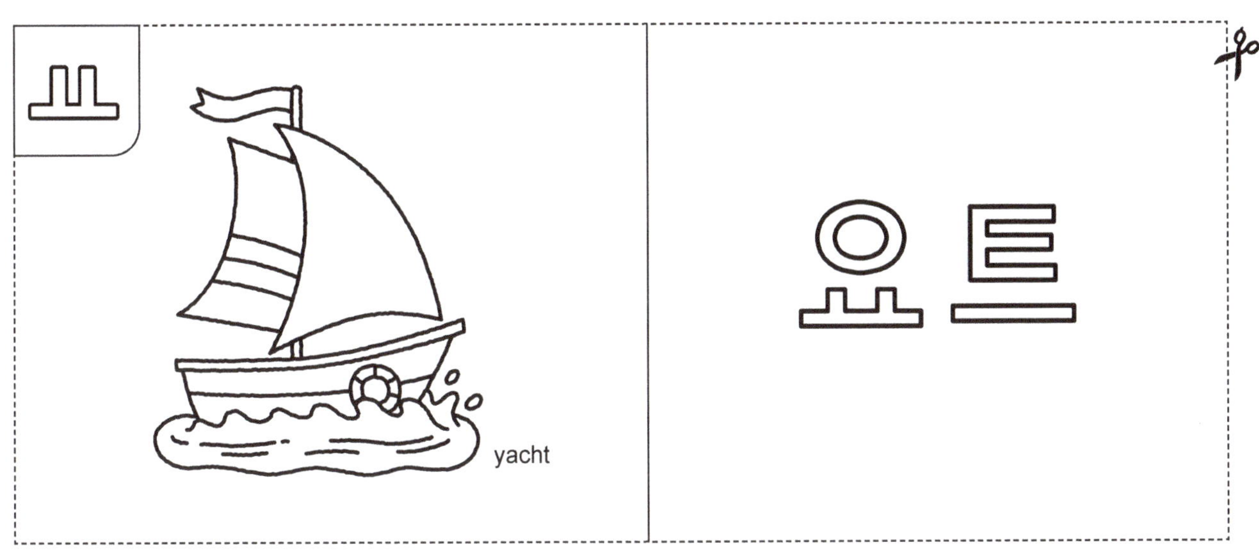

Korean Word Card

Color the ㅜ words and pictures, then cut and fold them to make Korean word cards.

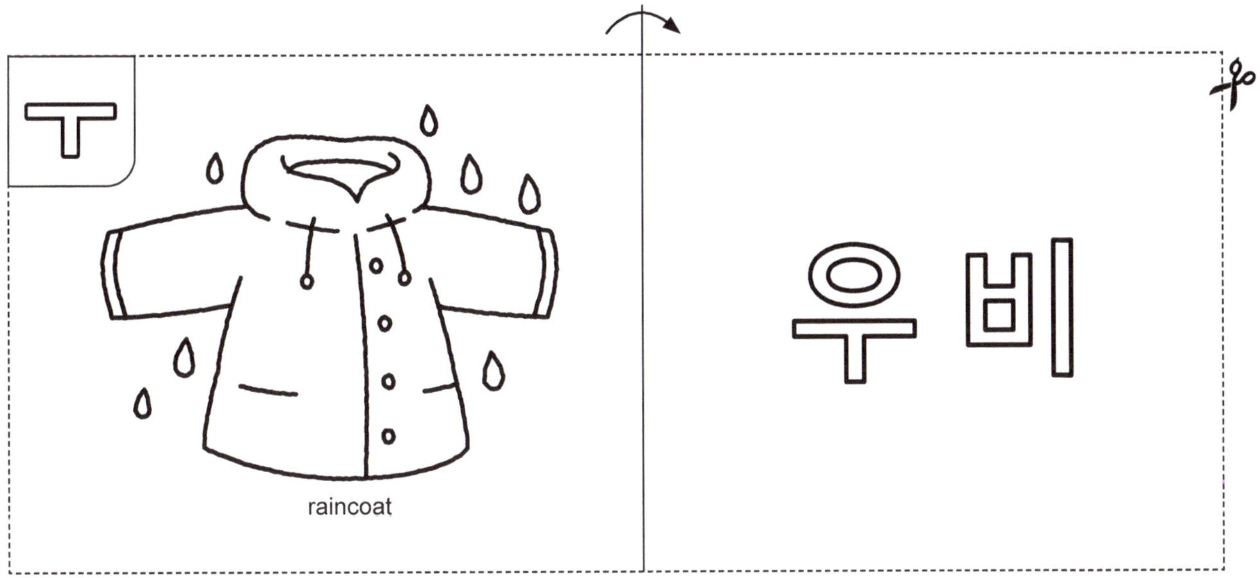

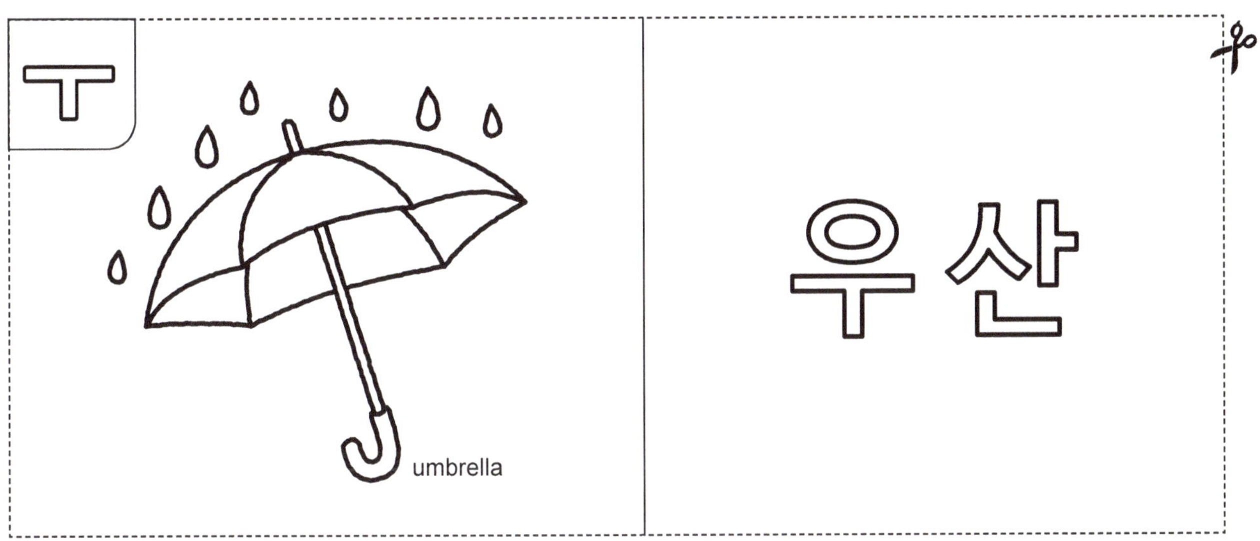

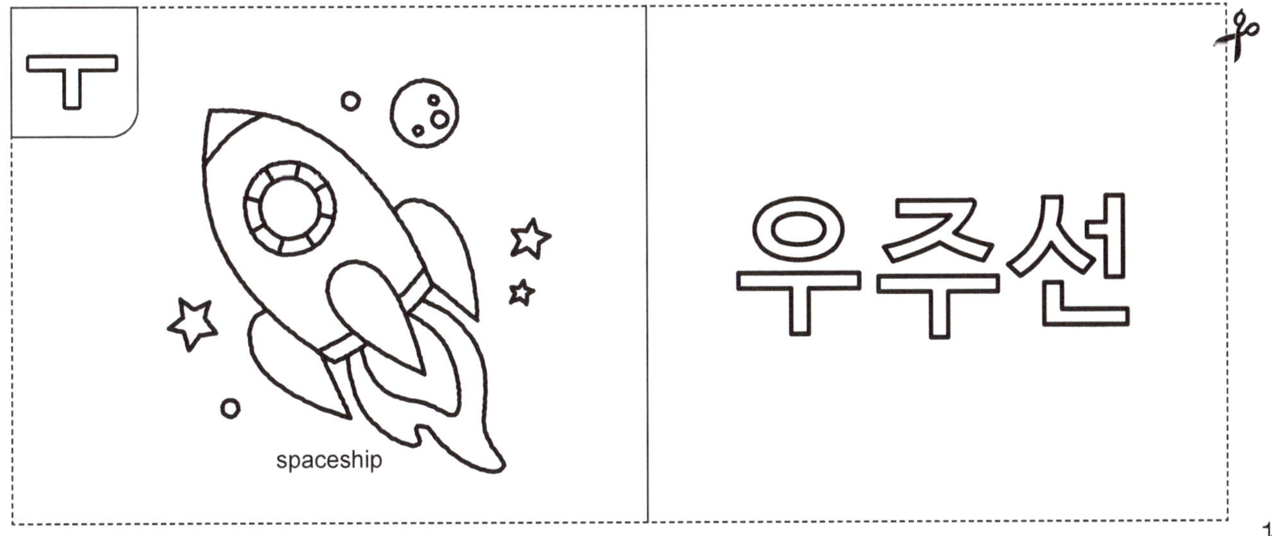

Korean Word Card

Color the ㅠ words and pictures, then cut and fold them to make Korean word cards.

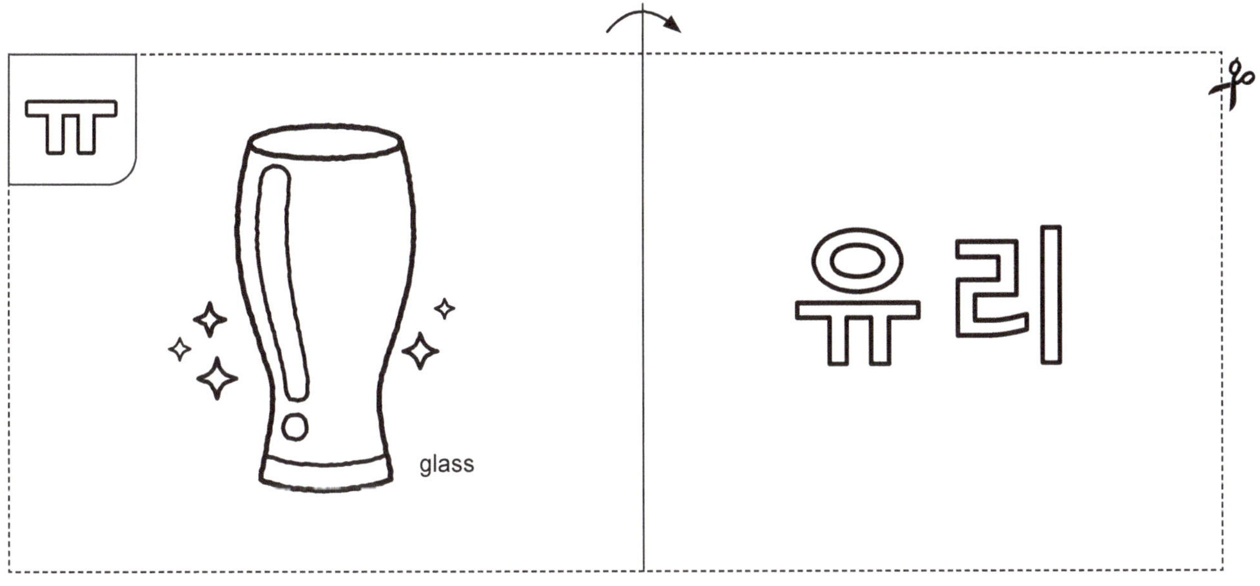

Come join us on our
YouTube channel!
youtube.com/@oorihangeul